FOUNDATIONS OF INFORMATION PRIVACY AND DATA PROTECTION

A Survey of Global Concepts, Laws and Practices

Peter P. Swire, CIPP/US

Kenesa Ahmad, CIPP/US

Managing Editor
Terry McQuay, CIPP/US, CIPP/C, CIPP/E, CIPP/G

An IAPP Publication

Cover design: Noelle Grattan, -ing designs, llc.
Copy editor: Sarah Weaver
Proofreader: Jane Anderson
Compositor: Ed Stevens, Ed Stevens Design
Indexer: Jan Bednarczuk, Jandex Indexing

ISBN 978-0-9795901-7-7
Library of Congress Control Number: 2012933904

About the IAPP

The International Association of Privacy Professionals (IAPP) is the largest and most comprehensive global information privacy community and resource, helping practitioners develop and advance their careers and organizations manage and protect their data.

The IAPP is a not-for-profit association founded in 2000 with a mission to define, support and improve the privacy profession globally through networking, education and certification. We are committed to providing a forum for privacy professionals to share best practices, track trends, advance privacy management issues, standardize the designations for privacy professionals, and provide education and guidance on opportunities in the field of information privacy.

The IAPP is responsible for developing and launching the first broad-based credentialing program in information privacy, the Certified Information Privacy Professional (CIPP). The CIPP remains the leading privacy certification for professionals who serve the data protection, information auditing, information security, legal compliance and/or risk management needs of their organizations. Today, many thousands of professionals worldwide hold a CIPP certification.

In addition, the IAPP offers a full suite of educational and professional development services and holds annual conferences that are recognized internationally as the leading forums for the discussion and debate of issues related to privacy policy and practice.

Contents

CHAPTER TWO
Geography: Privacy and Data Protection Regulation Around the World

CHAPTER THREE
Sectors of Privacy and Data Protection Law

CHAPTER FOUR
Information Security: Safeguarding Personal Information

CHAPTER FIVE
Online Privacy: Using Personal Information on Websites and Other Internet Technologies

List of Figures

Preface

I am writing this preface in March 2012, in the midst of what one might call the second wave of privacy for the Internet age.

The first wave occurred in the 1990s: The Internet saw its first commercial activities in 1993 and grew to over a billion users by 2000. In the European Union, the Data Protection Directive was finalized in 1995 and went into effect in 1998. In the United States, the Federal Trade Commission became active on privacy by 1996, pushing notably for companies and organizations to make enforceable privacy promises on their websites. By 1999, almost 90 percent of major commercial websites had privacy policies. Meanwhile, the Clinton administration supported legal protections for especially sensitive personal information, including the Children's Online Privacy Protection Act of 1998, the Gramm-Leach-Bliley Act for financial information in 1999, and the HIPAA medical privacy proposed rule of 1999 and final rule in 2000. I served as chief counselor for privacy in the U.S. government during this period, when the United States and EU addressed issues of trans-border data flows in the Safe Harbor agreement, signed in 2000.

The year 2000 also saw the formation of the Privacy Officers Association, now known as the International Association of Privacy Professionals. The time since has seen the remarkable growth of the IAPP, an instrumental force in assuring the professional, effective protection of personal information in private and public sector organizations. As discussed in Chapter 2 of this book, privacy and data protection laws spread to every continent in the following decade, with over 80 countries now having such laws on the books.

A second wave of privacy for the Internet age appears to be happening now. In January 2012, the European Commission proposed its regulation to make significant changes to the Data Protection Directive. This proposal comes during a period of intensive technological changes: (1) Social networks have expanded from a small scale to nearly a billion users in recent years; (2) mobile devices, including smartphones, are becoming pervasive, triggering numerous questions about how individuals' location information will be treated; and (3) online behavioral advertising has become a major focus of public attention, including in the Cookie Directive in the European Union and Do Not Track proposals in the United States. In this second wave, the Federal Trade

Commission has brought privacy enforcement actions against many of the most prominent Internet companies and has issued a major report calling for further change. The Obama administration in February 2012 announced support for a Consumer Privacy Bill of Rights, and is the first U.S. administration to call for general private sector privacy legislation. This combination of proposed changes in the EU and United States may well result in the biggest modifications to global privacy laws and practices in over a decade.

The work of privacy and data protection professionals today follows in the footsteps of pioneers such as Spiros Simitis, a creator of data protection in Europe, and Willis Ware, who was the chief drafter of the first set of fair information practices in the early 1970s. I would like to dedicate my own work in this book to Alan Westin, author of the 1967 classic *Privacy and Freedom* and director of the 1972 National Academy of Sciences report "Databanks in a Free Society: Computers, Record-Keeping, and Privacy." That report concluded with an explanation about why our work in this area is so important (and interesting):

> *Computers are here to stay. So are large organizations and the need for data. So is the American commitment to civil liberties. Equally real are the social cleavages and cultural reassessments that mark our era. Our task is to see that appropriate safeguards for the individual's rights to privacy, confidentiality, and due process are embedded in every major record system in the nation, particularly for the computerizing systems that promise to be the setting for most important organizational uses of information affecting individuals in the coming decades.*

Although the quotation mentions "the American commitment to civil liberties" and discusses the record systems in one nation, the challenges of privacy and data protection today are thoroughly global. Today, privacy is treated as a fundamental human right in the legal systems of many nations, and the rise of the Internet means that individuals and businesses daily send and receive personal information across borders. The global nature of the challenge is why *Foundations of Information Privacy and Data Protection* gives careful attention to privacy laws and practices globally, and not simply in the United States and European Union.

In closing, my particular thanks to co-author Kenesa Ahmad for her extensive and excellent work on this book. Thanks to Sol Bermann and all those who contributed to its 2007 predecessor. My appreciation as well to Marla Berry, Dick Soule and the others at IAPP who have worked on this project, and to Terry McQuay and those at Nymity and elsewhere who worked with him to complete the book you have before you.

Peter Swire, CIPP/US
March 2012

Acknowledgments

The book you hold in your hands, *Foundations of Information Privacy and Data Protection: A Survey of Global Concepts, Laws and Practices,* is the result of the evolution of the Certified Information Privacy Professional (CIPP) program into specific designations and a prerequisite Certification Foundation program.

We published *Information Privacy: Official Reference for the Certified Information Privacy Professional (CIPP)* in 2007 as our first textbook to support the CIPP program. We were fortunate to have Peter Swire and Sol Bermann as the authors of *Information Privacy.* Both continue to make important contributions to the privacy and data protection communities and it is their significant and impressive work on *Information Privacy* on which *Foundations of Information Privacy and Data Protection* is based.

I am most appreciative of our inaugural Certification Foundation Advisory Board for their guidance in shaping the Certification Foundation program. These distinguished board members represent a global perspective on privacy and data protection. Past and present members are:

Caroline Doulcet
Lawyer, Cabinet Gelly

Peggy Eisenhauer, CIPP/US
Founder and Principal, Privacy and Information Management Services P.C.

Hazel Grant
Partner, Bristows

Robert Gratchner, CIPP/US
Vice President, Privacy, AudienceScience

John Howie, CIPP/US, CIPP/IT
Chief Operating Officer, Cloud Security Alliance

Lucy McDonald, CIPP/C
Consultant, Information Privacy Network, Inc.

Charlene Wright Thomas, CIPP/G
Senior Advisor for Privacy Policy, Department of State

I am thankful and honored that Peter Swire accepted our invitation to update and revise portions of *Information Privacy* into a comprehensive and global textbook to support our Certification Foundation program. This excellent work is the result of many hours of research, writing and editing. We are very grateful for his time and commitment to this important text.

Thank you to Kenesa Ahmad, who worked closely with Peter throughout all phases of the researching and writing. Kenesa's careful analysis of the content has ensured that all concepts critical to the Certification Foundation program are discussed in the text.

There are many steps to converting a manuscript into a published text. Thank you to Caroline Doulcet, Peggy Eisenhauer, John Howie, Lucy McDonald, Terry McQuay and Charlene Thomas, who carefully reviewed the draft manuscript and offered suggestions for shaping it into a comprehensive and meaningful textbook.

My sincere gratitude to Terry McQuay and to members of his team at Nymity—Lara Hunt, John Jager, Camille McQuay, Meaghan McCluskey and Blaine Currie—for distilling the reviewers' comments and providing suggestions, research and writing to support the editing of the text into a final manuscript.

Thank you to Lindsay Allen and Colin Morrow, who provided feedback on the content and flow of the text and helped to research and validate the chapter notes, and to our copy editor, Sarah Weaver, for her attention to consistency, style and detail.

Finally, I'd like to acknowledge those people without whom the CIPP could not exist as it does today. I appreciate the generous support of the founding grantors of the initial CIPP program: Hewlett-Packard and Microsoft. The IAPP's original CIPP Advisory Board articulated the initial requirements for the CIPP and I thank this group for sharing their expertise and for providing guidance. Thank you to the contributors to our first CIPP textbook, *Information Privacy*—Dennis Becktell, Matt Beirlein, Margaret Betzel, Katy Delaney, Josh Deinsen, Peggy Eisenhauer, Jim Jordan, Barbara Lawler and Shannon Rogers.

The CIPP recognizes professionals in information privacy and data protection across industries and jurisdictions. Thank you for participating in the CIPP program. The IAPP continues to provide the privacy community with networking, education and certification opportunities to both support and improve this dynamic field. We look forward to seeing you at one of our events or programs.

Richard Soule, CIPP/E
Certification Director
International Association of Privacy Professionals

Introduction

I am proud to present you with this updated edition of our flagship resource for certification exam preparation.

When we published *Information Privacy*, our first certification textbook, in 2007, there was no EU Cookie Directive, U.S. HITECH Act or Mexican data protection law. Regulatory enforcement of privacy statutes was uncommon, and many were asking, "Where are the lawsuits?"

Much has changed since then. Today, privacy-related enforcement actions are common. So is litigation. Data privacy has become a competitive differentiator in the marketplace; privacy laws have become drivers to economic expansion in developing nations, and in 2011, world leaders put data protection on the agenda of the G8 Summit.

There is no question that data protection and privacy matters have grown in scope and sophistication. This textbook reflects the extensive developments that have occurred. Peter Swire, working with Kenesa Ahmad, has once again condensed key concepts into an impactful guide. Whether you are new to the field or work in an adjacent profession, I am certain you will find the foundational knowledge contained within these pages very useful to your work and career.

Thousands of professionals have used the content in this book to prepare for the Certification Foundation exam—the prerequisite test for our Certified Information Privacy Professional (CIPP) exam. Today, more than 3,100 individuals hold the CIPP/US credential. Thousands of others hold one or more of our other certification credentials—the CIPP/G (U.S. government), CIPP/C (Canada), CIPP/IT (information technology) and our newest—the CIPP/E (Europe). The data protection and privacy landscape has matured greatly. The professionals who maneuver within it have, too.

I hope you will find this book useful to both your work in the field and your preparation for the Certification Foundation exam. Demand for privacy-savvy professionals will continue to grow; your interest in this book sets you on a bright path. I applaud you for making this investment in your career and the profession.

J. Trevor Hughes, CIPP
President and CEO
International Association of Privacy Professionals

CHAPTER ONE

Common Principles and Approaches to Information Privacy and Data Protection

This chapter provides an introduction to protection of information about individuals. In the United States and other countries, laws in this area are known as **privacy law,** or sometimes data privacy or information privacy law. In the European Union (EU) and other countries, laws in this area are known as **data protection law.** The discussion introduces the relevant vocabulary and describes the common principles and approaches used throughout the world for information privacy and data protection.

1. Defining Privacy

In 1890, Samuel Warren and Louis Brandeis published "The Right to Privacy" in the *Harvard Law Review*, setting forth the essential definition of privacy as "the right to be left alone."[1] Both fundamental and concise, this definition underscored the personal and social dimensions of the concept that would linger long after publication of this landmark essay.

In the time since, numerous other individuals, organizations and world bodies have proposed their own privacy definitions. Privacy has been defined as the desire of people to freely choose the circumstances and degree to which individuals will expose their attitudes and behavior to others.[2] It has been connected to the human personality and used as a means to protect an individual's independence, dignity and integrity.[3]

More recently, privacy was defined in 1997 by the United Kingdom's Calcutt Committee as "[t]he right of the individual to be protected against intrusion into his personal life or affairs, or those of his family, by direct physical means or by publication of information."[4] The Australian Privacy Charter states that "[a] free and democratic society requires respect for the autonomy of individuals, and limits on the power of both state and private organizations to intrude on that autonomy."[5]

Establishing an understanding of how privacy is defined and categorized—as well as how it has emerged as a social concern—is critical to understanding data protection and privacy law as they have been established today in Europe, the United States and elsewhere around the world.

2. Classes of Privacy

While privacy can be defined in many ways, four areas of privacy are of particular interest with regard to data protection and privacy laws and practices.[6]

1. **Information privacy** is concerned with establishing rules that govern the collection and handling of personal information. Examples include financial information, medical information, government records and records of a person's activities on the Internet.

2. **Bodily privacy** is focused on a person's physical being and any invasion thereof. Such an invasion can take the form of genetic testing, drug testing or body cavity searches. It also encompasses issues such as birth control, abortion and adoption.

3. **Territorial privacy** is concerned with placing limits on the ability to intrude into another individual's environment. "Environment" is not limited to the home; it may be defined as the workplace or public space. Invasion into an individual's territorial privacy typically takes the form of monitoring such as video surveillance, ID checks and use of similar technology and procedures.

4. **Communications privacy** encompasses protection of the means of correspondence, including postal mail, telephone conversations, e-mail and other forms of communicative behavior and apparatus.

While some of these categories may interrelate, this reference text will focus primarily on the legal, technological and practical components of information privacy.

3. The Historical and Social Origins of Privacy

The concept of information privacy as a social concept is rooted in some of the oldest texts and cultures.[7] Privacy is referenced numerous times in the laws of classical Greece and in the Bible. The concept of the freedom from being watched has historically been recognized by Jewish law.[8] Privacy is similarly recognized in the Qur'an and in the sayings of Mohammed where there is discussion of the privacy of prayer as well as in the avoidance of spying or talking ill of someone behind their back.[9]

The legal protection of privacy rights has a similarly far-reaching history. In England, the Justices of the Peace Act, enacted in 1361, included provisions calling for the arrest of "peeping Toms" and eavesdroppers.[10]

In 1765, British Lord Camden protected the privacy of the home, striking down a warrant to enter the home and seize papers from it. He wrote, "We can safely say there is no law in this country to justify the defendants in what they have done; if there was, it would destroy all the comforts of society, for papers are often the dearest property any man can have."[11] Parliamentarian William Pitt shared this view, declaring that "[t]he poorest man may in his cottage bid defiance to all the force of the Crown. It may be frail: its roof may shake; the wind may blow through it; the storms may enter; the rain may enter—but the King of England cannot enter; all his forces dare not cross the threshold of the ruined tenement."[12]

In the ensuing centuries, other European countries advanced their own privacy protections. The Swedish Parliament enacted the Access to Public Records Act in 1776, requiring that information held by the government be used for legitimate purposes. In 1858, France prohibited the publication of private facts, with violators of the prohibition subject to strict fines.[13] The Norwegian Criminal Code prohibited publication of information that relates to an individual's personal or domestic affairs as early as 1889.[14]

In many parts of the world, modern privacy has arisen within the context of human rights. In December 1948, the General Assembly of the United Nations adopted and proclaimed the Universal Declaration of Human Rights.[15] This declaration formally announced that "[n]o one shall be subjected to arbitrary interference with his privacy, family, home or correspondence."[16] The statement was intended to encompass a wide range of conduct, as evidenced by Article 12 of the declaration, which describes both the territorial and the communications notions of privacy.

Also in 1948, the Organization of American States adopted the American Declaration of the Rights and Duties of Man.[17] This declaration predated the Universal Declaration of Human Rights by six months and conveyed a similar sentiment, providing that "[e]very person has the right to the protection of the law against abusive attacks upon . . . his private and family life." [18]

Human Rights and Data Protection

As a result of concerns that, in light of emerging technology, national legislation did not adequately protect the right to respect for private and family life set out in Article 8 of the European Convention for the Protection of Human Rights and Fundamental Freedoms, in the late 1960s the Council of Europe decided to establish a framework of specific principles and standards to prevent unfair collection and processing of personal information.

The Council of Europe published Recommendation 509 on Human Rights and Modern and Scientific Technological Developments, which was later built on to establish principles for the protection of personal data in automated data banks, with the objective of setting in motion the development of national legislation addressing these principles.

In 1950, the Council of Europe set forth the European Convention for the Protection of Human Rights and Fundamental Freedoms (ECHR).[19] This convention acknowledged the goals of the aforementioned Universal Declaration of Human Rights and sought to secure the recognition and observance of the rights stated by the United Nations. The convention provides that "[e]veryone has the right to respect for his private and family life, his home and his correspondence."[20] Article 8 of the treaty limits a public authority's interference with an individual's right to privacy, but acknowledges an exception for actions in accordance with the law that are necessary to preserve a democratic society.

4. Information Privacy, Data Protection and the Advent of Information Technology

Modern ideas about privacy have been decisively shaped by the rapid development of information technology (IT). Mainframe computers emerged by the 1960s to handle the data processing and storage needs of business, government, educational and other institutions. As hardware and software evolved, there were clear and large benefits to individuals and society, ranging from increased economic growth to easier communications for individuals. The unprecedented accumulation of personal data, and the resulting potential for increased surveillance, also triggered an acute interest in privacy practices and the privacy rights of individuals. A vivid image of the risk came from George Orwell's book *1984*, where the government kept citizens under surveillance at all times, warning them with the slogan "Big Brother is watching you." To prevent the creation of "Big Brother," there were increasing demands for formal rules to govern the collection and handling of personal information.

In response to this sort of concern, in 1970 the German state of Hesse enacted the first known modern data protection law. This German law was motivated in part by the growing potential of IT systems as well as an attempt to prevent a reoccurrence of the personal information abuses that took place under Hitler's Third Reich, before and during World War II. Such concerns were not confined to Germany, and over the next decade several European countries enacted national privacy laws of differing objectives and scope. The United States passed its first national privacy law in 1970, the Fair Credit Reporting Act, focused on the single sector of information about consumer credit.

5. Personal and Nonpersonal Information

For information privacy, a central issue is the extent to which information can be linked to a particular person. Aggregate or statistical information generally does not raise privacy compliance issues.

5.1 Personal Information

"Personal data" is defined in the EU as any and all data that relates to an identified or identifiable individual.[21] In the United States, the term "personally identifiable information (PII)" is generally used to define the information that is covered by privacy laws. In Canada, "personal information" is defined as information about an identifiable individual, but does not include certain business contact information.[22] And in Japan, "personal information" means information that relates to living individuals and that can identify specific individuals by name, date of birth or other description (including data that can be easily compared with other information and thereby used to identify specific individuals).[23]

Personal Information

This book uses the standard term personal information *when referring to what is known in various jurisdictions as personal data, personally identifiable information (PII), personal health information, employee personal information and so on. When discussing a specific law, this book will use the legal term contained in that law; for example,* personal data *is found in the EU Data Protection Directive, Argentina's Personal Data Protection Act, and Hong Kong's Personal Data (Privacy) Ordinance;* personal information *is used in Australia's Privacy Act and Canada's PIPEDA;* protected health information *appears in U.S. HIPAA.*

All of these definitions are similar. They include information about an identified individual, such as name and Social Security number or national identifier. They also include information about an "identified" or "identifiable" individual. For instance, street address, telephone number and e-mail address are generally considered sufficiently related to a particular person to count as "identifiable" information, within the scope of privacy protections. The definitions generally apply to both electronic and paper records.

Sensitive personal information is an important subset of personal information. The definition of what is considered sensitive may vary depending on jurisdiction and particular regulations. In Europe, for example, the EU Data Protection Directive calls sensitive personal information **special categories of data**, which refers to personal data revealing racial or ethnic origin, political opinions, religious or philosophical beliefs, trade union membership, or data concerning health or sex life.[24] However, other data can be considered sensitive in certain European countries and its use may be subject to strict rules—for example, processing of Social Security numbers or automatic processing of biometric data in France. In the United States, Social Security numbers and financial information are commonly treated as sensitive information, as are driver's license numbers and health information. In Canada, Schedule 1, Principle 4.3.4 of the Personal Information Protection and Electronic Documents Act (PIPEDA) notes that any information can be sensitive, depending on the context.[25] In almost all countries, health information is considered sensitive. In general, sensitive information will require additional privacy and security limitations to safeguard its collection, use and disclosure.

5.2 Nonpersonal Information

If the data elements used to identify the individual are removed, the remaining data becomes nonpersonal information, and privacy and data protection laws generally do not apply. Similar terms are "de-identified" or "anonymized" information. This type of information is frequently used for research, statistical or aggregate purposes. "Pseudonymized" data exists where information about individuals is retained under pseudonyms, such as a unique numerical code for each person.

The focus of privacy and data protection laws is generally on information about the individual, rather than about a corporation or other organization. In some instances, such as for a sole proprietorship or other small business, the information is so closely linked to an individual that it may be considered as personal information.

5.3 The Line Between Personal and Nonpersonal Information

The difference between personal and nonpersonal information depends on what is "identifiable"; the line between these two categories is not always clear, and regulators and courts in different jurisdictions may disagree on what counts as personal information.

Other Information Assets of an Organization

As part of their normal activities, organizations also may collect and generate information that by its nature would not be considered personal information, but is nevertheless a key part of the information assets of the organization. Examples of such information include:

- *Financial data*
- *Operational data*
- *Intellectual property*
- *Information about the organization's products and services*

Though not personal information, such information needs to be protected and secured to ensure its confidentiality.

Recital 26 of the EU Data Protection Directive states that "the principles of protection shall not apply to data rendered anonymous in such a way that the data subject is no longer identifiable." The regulators in the Article 29 Working Party have cautioned, however, that retraceably pseudonymized data may be considered information on individuals who are indirectly identifiable.[26] That is, the ability to retrace an individual's identity, even when masked, can mean that information is considered personal information and thus subject to data protection.

As an example of how different regimes have defined the line between personal and nonpersonal information, consider the IP (Internet protocol) address, the numbers that identify computers in communications over the Internet. The EU considers IP addresses "personal data," taking the view that IP addresses are "identifiable." A court in Ireland, however, determined that IP addresses did not constitute personal information.[27] In the United States, federal agencies operating under the Privacy Act do not consider IP addresses to be covered by the statute.[28] However, the Federal Trade Commission (FTC), an independent agency in the United States, has stated in connection with breaches of healthcare information that IP addresses are personal information.[29]

Assessing an Organization's Personal Information Responsibilities

The line between personal and nonpersonal information illustrates a critical first step in assessing an organization's personal information responsibilities—is the organization covered by a law or other obligation?

With globalization, information privacy professionals may need to determine when the laws of a particular jurisdiction apply. In addition, some laws apply only to particular sectors or types of information. The HIPAA medical privacy law in the United States, for instance, applies only to certain organizations ("covered entities") and certain information ("personal health information").

Changes in technology can also shift the line between personal and nonpersonal information. For instance, historically, IP addresses were usually "dynamic"—individuals would generally get a new IP address assigned by their Internet service provider each time they logged on to the Internet. Over time, more individuals have had "static" IP addresses, which stay the same for each computer device, linking the device more closely to an identifiable person. The next version of the Internet protocol (IPv6) uses a new numbering scheme that, by default, uses information about the computer to generate an IPv6 address, making it even easier to link devices (including smartphones) and their users.

6. Sources of Personal Information

Sometimes the same information about an individual is treated differently based on the source of the information. To illustrate this point, consider three sources of personal information: public records, publicly available information and nonpublic information.

1. **Public records** are information collected and maintained by a government entity and available to the general public. These government entities include the national, state/provincial and local governments. Public records laws vary considerably across jurisdictions.

   For instance, real estate records in some jurisdictions contain detailed information about ownership, assessed value, amount paid for the parcel, taxes imposed on the parcel and improvements. Making this information public has certain advantages, such as enabling a person who owns real estate to determine if the taxes assessed are fair relative to other parcels in the area. Other jurisdictions, by contrast, do not release such information, considering it to be private.

2. **Publicly available information** is information that is generally available to a wide range of persons. Some traditional examples are names and addresses in telephone books and information published in newspapers or other public media. Today, search engines are a major source for publicly available information.

3. **Nonpublic information** is not generally available or easily accessed due to law or custom. Examples of this type of data are medical records, financial information and adoption records. A company's customer or employee database usually contains nonpublic information.

Organizations should be alert to the possibility that the same information may be public record, publicly available and nonpublic. For example, a name and address may be a matter of public record (on a real estate deed), publicly available in the telephone book and included in nonpublic databases, such as in a healthcare patient file. To understand how to handle the name and address, one must understand the source that provided it—restrictions may apply to use of the name and address in the patient file, but not to public records or publicly available information.

7. Processing Personal Information

As introduced above, almost anything that someone may do with personal information might constitute "processing" under privacy and data protection laws. The term *processing* refers to the collection, recording, organization, storage, updating or modification, retrieval, consultation and use of personal information. It also includes the disclosure by transmission, dissemination or making available in any other form, linking, alignment or combination, blocking, erasure or destruction of personal information. The following common terms, first widely used in the EU, apply to data processing:

- **Data subject** is the individual about whom information is being processed, such as the patient at a medical facility, the employee of a company or the customer of a retail store.

- **Data controller** is an organization that has the authority to decide how and why personal information is to be processed. This entity is the focus of most obligations under privacy and data protection laws—it controls the use of personal information by determining the purposes for its use and the manner in which the information will be processed.[30] The data controller may be an individual or an organization that is legally treated as an individual, such as a corporation or partnership.

- **Data processor** is an individual or organization, often a third-party outsourcing service, that processes data on behalf of the data controller. A data controller might not have the employees or expertise in-house to do some types of activity, or might find it more efficient to get assistance from other organizations. For instance, a data controller may hire another organization to do accounting and back-office operations. The first data processor, in turn, might hire other organizations to act as data processors on its behalf, such as if a company providing back-office operations hired a subcontractor to manage its website. Each organization in the chain—from data controller, to data processor, to any subsequent data processor acting on behalf of the first data processor—is expected to act in a trusted way, doing operations that are consistent with the direction of the data controller. The data processors are not authorized to do additional data processing outside of the scope of what is permitted for the data controller itself.

8. Human Resources, Customers and Other Categories of Personal Information

Privacy professionals should be familiar with major categories of personal information in order to be alert to possible obligations. Employee and customer information are two major categories, although others exist. Chapter 3 discusses how privacy laws may vary by sector, including sectors such as healthcare, financial services, telecommunications, Internet privacy and government records. Privacy professionals should be aware that sector-specific laws and practices may exist for these sorts of personal information.

> *Customer Information*
>
> *The term* customer information *as used in this section includes customers and clients of private sector organizations, as well as individuals who receive services from public sector agencies.*

As a general matter, typical elements of personal information include:

- Name
- Gender
- Contact information (address, phone number, e-mail, etc.)
- Age and date of birth
- Marital status
- Other demographic information (such as income or education)
- Languages spoken

8.1 Human Resources Information

Chapter 2 discusses the difference between nations that have comprehensive data protection laws, such as those in the EU, and countries that do not. Comprehensive data protection laws treat employee and other human resources information under the general rules for personal information, while other countries may have specific obligations for human resources information.

Typical elements of human resources information include:

- Salary
- Job title
- Productivity and performance statistics
- Medical and pension benefits
- Employee evaluations

- Disabled, veteran or other relevant status
- Location information (e.g., collected via GPS)
- Nationality

Personal information may not be limited to data about current employees. For instance, a company may have personal information about applicants, former or retired employees, dependents and beneficiaries, contractors, volunteers and vendors. Personal information may also be collected for purposes such as conducting investigations into employee misconduct.

8.2 Customer Information

Where an organization deals with individuals (including patients), it often has detailed personal information about them. Along with contact and demographic information discussed above, customer information may include:

- Purchase history
- Other history of interactions, such as visits to a website or physical facility
- Information about leads or prospects
- Former customers
- Market research participants
- Voice recording of telephone calls
- Citizens or others who receive social security, health or other benefits from the government
- Tax records and other records about individuals held by the government

8.3 Other Information

Personal information can exist in settings beyond human resource and customer information. For instance, a government agency may process personal information to investigate crimes or protect national security. Private companies may gather data about individuals who are not customers for a range of business reasons, such as to identify members of the press and other individuals important to the company's goals. The privacy professional should be alert to the possibility that personal information is maintained by an organization outside of the human resources and customer record systems.

9. Privacy Policy and Notice Defined

A **privacy policy** is an internal statement that governs an organization's or entity's handling practices of personal information. It is directed at the users of the personal information. A privacy policy instructs employees on the collection and use of the data, as well as any specific rights the data subjects may have.

> ### *Privacy Policy as a Privacy Notice*
>
> *It is common to use the organization's privacy policy as a privacy notice. For example, many organizations will place their privacy policy on their website and use it as a privacy notice in lieu of developing a separate document.*

A **privacy notice** is a statement made to a data subject that describes how the organization collects, uses, retains and discloses personal information. A privacy notice is sometimes referred to as a privacy statement, a fair processing statement or a privacy policy.

Privacy notices serve at least two important purposes: consumer education and organizational accountability. They can provide individuals with the information needed to understand how an organization will process information. They also provide regulators and organizational managers with a benchmark against which actual organizational practices are judged.

Privacy notices come in many forms; the following are some common examples:

- Contracts (e.g., cardholder agreements or employment contracts) may specify how a company may handle personal information.
- Application forms (e.g., job applications or applications for services such as a bank account) may indicate how personal information contained within the application will be treated.
- Specific web pages may be dedicated to privacy, often linked to from the home page or landing page of the website.
- Terms of use (e.g., the terms governing a user's participation in an online service or social network) may establish rules around personal information handling.
- Icons (e.g., the Interactive Advertising Bureau's Advertising Option Icon, along with accompanying language) would indicate how data is collected and used for behavioral advertising.
- Signs may serve as privacy notices—for example, when entering an area captured by closed-circuit television (CCTV) cameras, a sign may include text such as "premises under surveillance" and/or icons, such as a picture of a video camera.
- Brochures may explain privacy policies—for example, a healthcare provider may provide new patients with an information sheet explaining how health information is collected, used and disclosed.

10. Information Risk Management

An important role for the privacy professional is to manage risk for the organization. Improper handling of personal information can lead to a range of problems and costs.

10.1 Privacy Impact on Organizational Risk

Privacy is multifaceted. It is a personal issue, a social issue, a legal issue and a business issue. Organizations face the challenge of effectively managing compliance, expectations and risk across increasingly complex and geographically diverse enterprises.

Some of the main drivers for organizations to protect information include compliance with laws, regulations and contracts; prevention of data breaches; and avoidance of enforcement actions or lawsuits. Organizations must also counter identity theft and fraud, as well as manage other business risks to its brand and reputation.

Other drivers of risk include meeting customer expectations and staying up to date with evolving technologies. These technologies include Internet-based services, enterprise resource planning systems and customer relationship management technologies. Organizations must also meet the demands of outsourcing, off-shoring and extended global enterprises, and must consider process harmonization as well as cost reduction.

Data Destruction

Many data breaches have resulted when personal information was not secured while awaiting destruction (e.g., kept in unlocked rooms or transferred to a vendor for destruction in an unsecure manner) or was destroyed in an insecure manner (e.g., data storage devices not electronically wiped or degaussed to a sufficient degree, or paper documents not shredded or pulped before being placed in a rubbish bin).

Data needs to be protected throughout its life cycle, from collection to destruction. Appropriate methods of destruction vary based on the type and sensitivity of personal information involved.

10.2 Categories of Safeguards

Effective management of information requires three kinds of safeguards: administrative, technical and physical.

- **Administrative safeguards** include the management measures that an organization takes to assure proper management of personal information. For instance, these measures include policies that employees are expected to follow with respect to personal information, such as rules about which employees are permitted access. They include other privacy and security policies, such as an organization's announcement in a privacy policy about when personal data can be transferred to third parties.

- **Technical safeguards** refer to the technological measures that an organization implements to manage personal information. For example, an authentication system may require passwords or other technical measures before an individual can access data. Organizations may use encryption and other technical tools to prevent unauthorized users from being able to read and understand information even if they gain access to it.

- **Physical safeguards** are a third essential component of the overall protection of information. For traditional paper documents, locks can secure the physical filing cabinets. Physical safeguards are also important for records stored in electronic format, such as preventing loss or theft of a laptop computer, or preventing access to a computing facility where an unauthorized user might be able to access and copy information.

These three types of safeguards reinforce each other. For instance, administrative safeguards may state that an employee should not download patient medical files to a laptop. Technical safeguards may provide for the encryption of data stored on a laptop, making unauthorized access difficult even if it is lost or stolen. Physical safeguards can include a physical lock on a computer so that it cannot be removed from an office.

10.3 Information Life Cycle Principles

The following principles track the information life cycle, from its collection and use through its storage or even disclosure. Generally, these principles place obligations or limitations on the collection, use, disclosure, storage and destruction of personal information.

- **Collection.** There should be limits to the collection of personal data; data should be collected by lawful and fair means and should be collected, where appropriate, with the knowledge or consent of the subject. Collection should be limited to an identified purpose and compatible uses; it should be proportionate and executed through fair and lawful means. Collection from third parties should also be considered.

- **Use.** Organizations should limit the use of personal information to the purposes identified in the notice and for which the individual has provided implicit or explicit consent.

- **Disclosure.** The organization discloses personal information to third parties only for the purposes identified in the notice and for which the individual has provided implicit or explicit consent. Rights of the data subject should be maintained even on transfer of the information to other parties. Other requirements should be conveyed to third-party controllers and processors. New purposes and uses may be subject to consent.

- **Storage and destruction.** The organization should retain personal information only for as long as necessary to fulfill the stated purpose. Data not retained should be securely disposed, returned or destroyed.

10.4 Privacy Risk Assessments

There are many ways for organizations to manage information risk. In the context of personal information, here are some common approaches.

Privacy impact assessments (PIAs) are checklists or tools to ensure that a personal information system is evaluated for privacy risks and designed with life cycle principles in mind. A PIA should be completed before implementation of the privacy project, product or service, and should be ongoing through its deployment. The PIA should identify these attributes of the data collected: what information is collected, why it is collected, the intended use of the information, with whom the information is shared, and the consent and choice rights of the data subjects. The PIA should be used to assess new systems, significant changes to existing systems, operational policies and procedures, and intended use of the information. PIAs should also be used before, during and after mergers and acquisitions. An effective PIA evaluates the sufficiency of privacy practices and policies with respect to existing legal, regulatory and industry standards, and maintains consistency between policy and practice.

Privacy assessments/audits are reviews of an organization's compliance with its privacy policies and procedures, applicable laws, regulations, service-level agreements, standards adopted by the entity and other contracts. The assessment or audit measures how closely the organization's practices align with its legal obligations and stated policies, and may rely on subjective information, such as employee interviews/questionnaires and complaints received, or on objective standards, such as information system logs or training attendance and test scores. Audits and assessments may be conducted internally by an audit function or externally by third parties. It is also common in some jurisdictions for the privacy/data protection officer to conduct assessments. The results of the assessment or audit are documented for management sign-off and analyzed to develop recommendations for improvement and a remediation plan. The issues and vulnerabilities noted are then monitored to ensure appropriate corrective action is taken on a timely basis. While assessments and audits may be conducted on a regular basis, they may also arise ad hoc as the result of a privacy or security event or a request from an enforcement authority.

Privacy by Design is the concept that organizations should build privacy directly into technology, systems and practices at the design phase to ensure privacy from the outset. Originating in the mid-1990s by the Information and Privacy Commissioner of Ontario, the principle has gained recognition around the globe, including from the U.S. Federal Trade Commission[31] and the European Commission (where the concept is also known as data protection by design or by default). Privacy by Design, as set forth by the Privacy Commissioner of Ontario, consists of seven foundational principles:[32]

1. **Proactive not Reactive; Preventative not Remedial.** Privacy by Design anticipates and prevents privacy-invasive events before they happen, rather than waiting for privacy risks to materialize.

2. **Privacy as the Default Setting.** No action is required by individuals to maintain their privacy; it is built into the system by default. This concept has been introduced in the European Commission's draft regulation to reform data protection.[33]

3. **Privacy Embedded into Design.** Privacy is an essential component of the core functionality being designed and delivered. The FTC has adopted this principle in its proposed consumer privacy framework, calling for companies to promote consumer privacy throughout the organization and at every stage of product development.[34]

4. **Full Functionality—Positive-Sum, not Zero-Sum.** Privacy by Design seeks to accommodate all legitimate interests and objectives, rather than making unnecessary trade-offs.

5. **End-to-End Security—Full Life Cycle Protection.** Strong security measures are essential to privacy, from start to finish of the life cycle of data. This is another principle the FTC has adopted in its proposed consumer privacy framework.[35]

6. **Visibility and Transparency—Keep It Open.** Component parts and operations remain visible to users and providers alike. Stakeholders are assured that the business practice or technology is operating according to stated promises and objectives.

7. **Respect for User Privacy—Keep It User-Centric.** The interests of individuals are prioritized in the offerings.

11. Fair Information Practices

Since the 1970s, **fair information practices** (FIPs), sometimes called fair information privacy practices or principles, have been a significant means for organizing the multiple individual rights and organizational responsibilities that exist with respect to personal information. The precise definitions of FIPs have varied over time and by geographic location; nonetheless, strong similarities exist for the major themes. In practice, there are various exceptions to the clear statements provided here, and the degree to which the FIPs are legally binding.

Important codifications of FIPs include:

- The 1973 U.S. Department of Health, Education and Welfare Fair Information Practice Principles

- The 1980 Organisation for Economic Co-operation and Development Guidelines Governing the Protection of Privacy and Transborder Data Flows of Personal Data (OECD Guidelines)

- The 1981 Council of Europe Convention for the Protection of Individuals with Regard to the Automatic Processing of Personal Data (COE Convention). This convention to a significant degree was codified in the 1995 EU Data Protection Directive

- The Asia-Pacific Economic Cooperation (APEC), which in 2004 agreed to a Privacy Framework

- The 2009 Madrid Resolution—International Standards on the Protection of Personal Data and Privacy

11.1 Overview of Fair Information Practices

Rights of Individuals

- **Notice.** Organizations should provide notice about their privacy policies and procedures, and should identify the purpose for which personal information is collected, used, retained and disclosed.

- **Choice and consent.** Organizations should describe the choices available to individuals and should get implicit or explicit consent with respect to the collection, use, retention and disclosure of personal information. Consent is often considered especially important for disclosures of personal information to other data controllers.

- **Data subject access.** Organizations should provide individuals with access to their personal information for review and update.

Opt In and Opt Out

Two central concepts of choice are "opt in" and "opt out."
- **Opt in** *means an individual actively affirms that information can be shared with third parties (e.g., an individual checks a box stating that she wants her information to go to another organization).*
- **Opt out** *means that, in the absence of action by the individual, information can be shared with third parties (e.g., unless the individual checks a box to opt out, her information can go to another organization).*

Controls on the Information

- **Information security.** Organizations should use reasonable administrative, technical and physical safeguards to protect personal information against unauthorized access, use, disclosure, modification and destruction.

- **Information quality.** Organizations should maintain accurate, complete and relevant personal information for the purposes identified in the notice.

Information Life Cycle

- **Collection.** Organizations collect personal information only for the purposes identified in the notice.

- **Use and retention.** Organizations should limit the use of personal information to the purposes identified in the notice and for which the individual has provided implicit or explicit consent. Organizations should also retain personal information only as long as necessary to fulfill the stated purpose.

- **Disclosure.** Organizations should disclose personal information to third parties only for the purposes identified in the notice and with the implicit or explicit consent of the individual.

Management

- **Management and administration.** Organizations should define, document, communicate and assign accountability for their privacy policies and procedures.

- **Monitoring and enforcement.** Organizations should monitor compliance with their privacy policies and procedures and have procedures to address privacy-related complaints and disputes.

11.2 U.S. Health, Education and Welfare Advisory Committee FIPs (1973)

The fair information practices used widely today date back to a 1973 report by the U.S. Department of Health, Education and Welfare Advisory Committee on Automated Systems.[36] The original Code of Fair Information Practices provided:

- There must be no personal data record-keeping systems whose very existence is secret.

- There must be a way for a person to find out what information about the person is in a record and how it is used.

- There must be a way for a person to prevent information about the person that was obtained for one purpose from being used or made available for other purposes without the individual's consent.

- There must be a way for a person to correct or amend a record of identifiable information about the person.

- Any organization creating, maintaining, using or disseminating records of identifiable personal data must assure the reliability of the data for its intended use and must take precautions to prevent misuse of the data.

Modern privacy law builds on important international agreements, including the OECD Guidelines.

11.3 OECD Guidelines (1980)

In 1980, the Organisation for Economic Co-operation and Development, an international organization that originally included the United States and European countries but has since expanded, published a set of privacy principles entitled "Guidelines Governing the Protection of Privacy and Transborder Data Flows of Personal Data."[37] The OECD Guidelines are perhaps the most widely recognized framework for fair information practices, and have been endorsed by the U.S. Federal Trade Commission and many other government organizations.[38] The Guidelines provide a privacy framework:

> *Collection Limitation Principle. There should be limits to the collection of personal data and any such data should be obtained by lawful and fair means and, where appropriate, with the knowledge or consent of the data subject.*

Data Quality Principle. *Personal data should be relevant to the purposes for which they are to be used, and, to the extent necessary for those purposes, should be accurate, complete and kept up-to-date.*

Purpose Specification Principle. *The purposes for which personal data are collected should be specified not later than at the time of data collection and the subsequent use limited to the fulfillment of those purposes or such others as are not incompatible with those purposes and as are specified on each occasion of change of purpose.*

Use Limitation Principle. *Personal data should not be disclosed, made available or otherwise used for purposes other than those specified in accordance with [the Purpose Specification Principle] except (a) with the consent of the data subject; or (b) by the authority of law.*

Security Safeguards Principle. *Personal data should be protected by reasonable security safeguards against such risks as loss or unauthorized access, destruction, use, modification or disclosure of data.*

Openness Principle. *There should be a general policy of openness about developments, practices and policies with respect to personal data. Means should be readily available of establishing the existence and nature of personal data, and the main purposes of their use, as well as the identity and usual residence of the data controller.*

Individual Participation Principle. *An individual should have the right: (a) to obtain from a data controller, or otherwise, confirmation of whether or not the data controller has data relating to him; (b) to have communicated to him, data relating to him, within a reasonable time, at a charge, if any, that is not excessive, in a reasonable manner, and in a form that is readily intelligible to him; (c) to be given reasons if a request made under subparagraphs (a) and (b) is denied, and to be able to challenge such denial; and (d) to challenge data relating to him and, if the challenge is successful to have the data erased, rectified, completed or amended.*

Accountability Principle. *A data controller should be accountable for complying with measures which give effect to the principles stated above.*

11.4 Council of Europe Convention (1981) and European Union Data Protection Directive (1995)

In 1981, the Council of Europe passed the Convention for the Protection of Individuals with Regard to the Automatic Processing of Personal Data (COE Convention).[39] The convention was broadly similar to the OECD Guidelines, and its principles were important contributors to national data protection laws in Europe in the 1980s and 1990s.[40]

The COE Convention and OECD Guidelines provided stepping stones toward uniform data protection throughout Europe. By the early 1990s, however, there were still significant differences among the privacy laws of the individual European nations.[41] Citizens of these nations were subject to varying levels of privacy protection. Importantly, the nonuniform laws resulted in data transmission problems within the EU, in violation of the EU's efforts to provide an integrated common market for economic activity.

Problems arose especially in connection with trans-border data flows. Many of the national laws set restrictions on trans-border flows of personal information, based on the principle that an individual's personal information should not receive reduced protection if it is transferred to another country. Some national laws required an individual or business that sought to export personal data to get consent from the data subject or approval from the originating country's authorities.[42] Upon export, public officials bore the responsibility of assuring that the information that was transported did not lose the protections it would be afforded within the originating country.

The **European Union Data Protection Directive** was drafted, at least in part, in response to these problems of trans-border data flows. The Directive was adopted in 1995 and went into effect in 1998. It directed each member state of the EU to adopt privacy laws that were "equivalent" to each other in providing protection of personal information. Although some variation continued among national laws, export was permitted freely between all members of the European Union, as well as other countries that had "adequate" privacy protection. The Directive thus sought to achieve twin goals: (1) a unified economic market within the European Union, permitting flows of personal information among the member states, and (2) strong overall protection of privacy within the EU. As discussed further in Chapter 2, a number of countries that are not members of the EU have since adopted laws that are similar to the requirements of the EU Directive. In early 2012, the European Commission proposed a draft regulation to update and modify the Directive, although a series of procedural steps will be required before it can enter into force. If and when such a regulation is adopted, its new provisions are likely to have an important effect on data protection requirements both within and outside of the EU.

11.5 APEC Privacy Framework (2004)

The Asia-Pacific Economic Cooperation (APEC) is a multinational organization with 21 Pacific coast members in Asia and the Americas. Unlike the EU, the APEC organization operates under nonbinding agreement. It was established in 1989 to enhance economic growth for the region.

In February 2003, the APEC Privacy Subgroup was established under the auspices of the Electronic Commerce Steering Group in order to develop a framework for privacy practices. This framework was designed to provide support to APEC-member economic legislation that would both protect individual interests and ensure the continued economic development of all APEC member economies.

The APEC Privacy Framework was approved by the APEC ministers in November 2004.[43] It contains nine information privacy principles that generally mirror the OECD Guidelines, but in some areas are more explicit about exceptions. The APEC privacy principles spelled out in the framework are:

1. ***Preventing Harm.*** *Recognizing the interests of the individual to legitimate expectations of privacy, personal information protection should be designed to prevent the*

misuse of such information. Further, acknowledging the risk that harm may result from such misuse of personal information, specific obligations should take account of such risk and remedial measures should be proportionate to the likelihood and severity of the harm threatened by the collection, use and transfer of personal information.

*2. **Notice**. Personal information controllers should provide clear and easily accessible statements about their practices and policies with respect to personal information that should include:*

a) the fact that personal information is being collected;

b) the purposes for which personal information is collected;

c) the types of persons or organizations to whom personal information might be disclosed;

d) the identity and location of the personal information controller, including information on how to contact it about its practices and handling of personal information; and,

e) the choices and means the personal information controller offers individuals for limiting the use and disclosure of, and for accessing and correcting, their personal information.

All reasonably practicable steps shall be taken to ensure that such information is provided either before or at the time of collection of personal information. Otherwise, such information should be provided as soon after as is practicable.

It may not be appropriate for personal information controllers to provide notice regarding the collection and use of publicly available information.

*3. **Collection Limitation**. The collection of personal information should be limited to information that is relevant to the purposes of collection and any such information should be obtained by lawful and fair means, and, where appropriate, with notice to, or consent of, the individual concerned.*

*4. **Uses of Personal Information**. Personal information collected should be used only to fulfill the purposes of collection and other compatible purposes except:*

a) with the consent of the individual whose personal information is collected;

b) when necessary to provide a service or product requested by the individual; or

c) by the authority of law and other legal instruments, proclamations and pronouncements of legal effect.

*5. **Choice**. Where appropriate, individuals should be provided with clear, prominent, easily understandable, accessible and affordable mechanisms to exercise choice in relation to the collection, use and disclosure of their personal information. It may not be appropriate for personal information controllers to provide these mechanisms when collecting publicly available information.*

6. ***Integrity of Personal Information.*** *Personal information should be accurate, complete and kept up-to-date to the extent necessary for the purposes of use.*

7. ***Security Safeguards.*** *Personal information controllers should protect personal information that they hold with appropriate safeguards against risks, such as loss or unauthorized access to personal information, or unauthorized destruction, use, modification or disclosure of information or other misuses. Such safeguards should be proportional to the likelihood and severity of the harm threatened, the sensitivity of the information and the context in which it is held, and should be subject to periodic review and reassessment.*

8. ***Access and Correction.*** *Individuals should be able to:*

    a) obtain from the personal information controller confirmation of whether or not the personal information controller holds personal information about them;

    b) have communicated to them, after having provided sufficient proof of their identity, personal information about them;

        i.   within a reasonable time;

        ii.   at a charge, if any, that is not excessive;

        iii.   in a reasonable manner; and,

        iv.   in a form that is generally understandable;

    c) challenge the accuracy of information relating to them and, if possible and as appropriate, have the information rectified, completed, amended or deleted.

Such access and opportunity for correction should be provided except where:

    (i)   the burden or expense of doing so would be unreasonable or disproportionate to the risks to the individual's privacy;

    (ii)   the information should not be disclosed due to legal, security or commercial proprietary reasons; or,

    (iii)   the information privacy of persons other than the individual would be violated.

If a request under (a) or (b) or a challenge under (c) is denied, the individual should be provided with reasons why and be able to challenge such denial.

9. ***Accountability.*** *A personal information controller should be accountable for complying with measures that give effect to the principles stated above. When personal information is to be transferred to another person or organization, whether domestically or internationally, the personal information controller should exercise due diligence and take reasonable steps to ensure that the recipient person or organization will protect the information consistently with these principles.*

11.6 Madrid Resolution (2009)

In 2009, the Madrid Resolution was approved by the independent data protection and privacy commissioners (not the governments themselves) at the annual International Conference of Data Protection and Privacy Commissioners, held in Madrid, Spain.[44] There were dual purposes for the Madrid Resolution–International Standards on the Protection of Personal Data and Privacy: to define a set of principles and rights guaranteeing (1) the effective and internationally uniform protection of privacy with regard to the processing of personal data and (2) the facilitation of the international flows of personal data needed in a globalized world.

The resolution has several basic principles:

- **Principle of lawfulness and fairness.** Personal data must be fairly processed, respecting the applicable national legislation as well as the rights and freedoms of individuals, and any processing that gives rise to unlawful or arbitrary discrimination against the data subject shall be deemed unfair.

- **Purpose specification principle.** Processing of personal data should be limited to the fulfillment of the specific, explicit and legitimate purposes of the responsible person; processing that is noncompatible with the purposes for which personal data was collected requires the unambiguous consent of the data subject.

- **Proportionality principle.** Processing of personal data should be limited to such processing as is adequate, relevant and not excessive in relation to the purposes, and reasonable efforts should be made to limit processing to the minimum necessary.

- **Data quality.** The responsible person should at all times ensure that personal data is accurate, sufficient and kept up to date in such a way as to fulfill the purposes for which it is processed, and the period of retention of the personal data shall be limited to the minimum necessary. Personal data no longer necessary to fulfill the purposes that legitimized its processing must be deleted or rendered anonymous.

- **Openness principle.** The responsible person shall provide to the data subjects, as a minimum, information about the responsible person's identity, the intended purpose of processing, the recipients to whom their personal data will be disclosed and how data subjects may exercise their rights. When data is collected directly from the data subject, this information must be provided at the time of collection, unless it has already been provided. When data is not collected directly from the data subject, the responsible person must inform him/her about the source of personal data. This information must be provided in an intelligible form, using clear and plain language, in particular for any processing addressed specifically to minors.

- **Accountability.** The responsible person shall take all the necessary measures to observe the principles and obligations set out in the resolution and in the applicable national legislation and have the necessary internal mechanisms in place for demonstrating such observance both to data subjects and to the supervisory authorities in the exercise of their powers.

12. Privacy or Data Protection Officers and Offices

Germany has required a data protection officer (DPO) for many companies since the early 1990s.[45] An increasing number of laws around the world require organizations to have one or more individuals responsible for privacy and data protection issues. Apart from such legal requirements, a large and growing number of other organizations are deciding to appoint a privacy or data protection officer, or create a privacy and data protection function within the organization. Signs of the importance of the privacy professional function include the growth of the International Association of Privacy Professionals since its creation in 2000, the number of people taking Certified Information Privacy Professional examinations and the development of an increasing range of CIPP certifications over time.

> ### Privacy or Data Protection Officers Under the Law
>
> Many national laws in EU countries require the appointment of a data protection officer (DPO), subject to factors such as number of employees in the organization. In some countries, such as Germany, the requirements for the DPO are spelled out in fairly specific terms. These detailed requirements stand in contrast to those of other jurisdictions (e.g., New Zealand or Canada) where requirements to appoint one or more individuals with responsibility for privacy are less specific. In the U.S., covered entities under the HIPAA medical privacy rule must appoint a privacy officer, but many other organizations do so without a legal requirement.

The location of privacy professionals within an organization varies considerably. Many privacy and data protection officers are part of a legal or compliance department. In other organizations, however, the officer may reside in marketing, IT or human resources, depending on the nature of the organization. In larger organizations, it is common to have a team that draws on multiple areas of expertise, including law, technology, marketing and other functions.

The privacy or data protection officer's responsibilities vary depending on the organization's risk and available resources. Officers are generally responsible to senior management for ensuring that the organization complies with privacy and data protection laws. Officers often monitor and report to both internal and external stakeholders about the organization's activities relating to privacy.

Reflecting the variation among organizations, privacy professionals fill a wide range of functions, including the following:[46]

1. **Governance structure.** Assure that there are individuals responsible for accountable management, data privacy policy and management reporting procedures.

2. **Personal data inventory.** Maintain an inventory of the location of personal information.

3. **Data privacy policies.** Maintain data privacy policies for the organization that meet legal requirements and operational risk tolerances.

4. **Operational policies and procedures.** Maintain operational policies and procedures consistent with data privacy policy, legal requirements and operational risk management.

5. **Ongoing training and awareness.** Assure ongoing training and awareness to promote compliance with data privacy policy and to mitigate operational risks.

6. **Security controls.** Maintain an information security program based on legal requirements and ongoing risk assessments.

7. **Contracts.** Create and maintain contracts and agreements with third parties and affiliates consistent with data privacy policy, legal requirements and operational risk tolerances.

Figure 1-1: Responsible Management Processes for Data Privacy Compliance

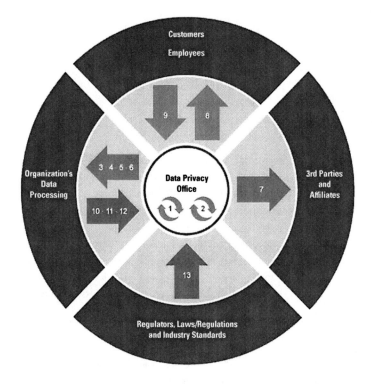

The numbers in the figure correspond to the numbered descriptions of privacy professional functions.
Used with permission from Nymity Inc.

8. **Notices.** Create and maintain notices to individuals consistent with the data privacy policy, legal requirements and operational risk tolerances.

9. **Inquiries, complaints and disputes.** Maintain effective procedures and track interactions with individuals about their personal data.

10. **New operational practices**. Monitor organizational practices to identify new processes or material changes in existing processes and apply the principles of Data Privacy by Design.

11. **Data privacy breaches.** Maintain an effective breach management program.

12. **Data handling practices.** Verify that operational practices comply with the data privacy policy and operational policies and procedures.

13. **Track external developments.** Track new compliance requirements, expectations and best practices.

13. Summary

This chapter has introduced key terminology about privacy and data protection laws and policies. It traced the history of these topics and the continued growth of legal requirements to accompany the evolution of information technology since the 1960s. Similar but not identical forms of fair information practices have been the basis of privacy and data protection laws in numerous countries around the globe, as discussed further in Chapter 2. As legal requirements have increased, the number of data protection and privacy professionals has grown rapidly, and their role has expanded in many organizations.

Endnotes

1 Samuel Warren and Louis Brandeis, "The Right to Privacy," *Harv. L. Rev.* 4 (1890): 193, http://groups. csail.mit.edu/mac/classes/6.805/articles/privacy/Privacy_brand_warr2.html. There are numerous sources of legal privacy, including tort privacy (Warren and Brandeis' original conception), Fourth Amendment privacy, First Amendment privacy, fundamental-decision privacy and state constitutional privacy. Ken Gormley, "One Hundred Years of Privacy," *Wis. L. Rev.* 1335 (1992), http://cyber.law. harvard.edu/privacy/Gormley--100%20Years%20of%20Privacy.htm.

2 Alan F. Westin, *Privacy and Freedom* (New York: Atheneum, 1967).

3 Edward J. Bloustein, "Privacy as an Aspect of Human Dignity: An Answer to Dean Prosser," *39 N.Y.U. L. Rev.* 962, 971 (1964): 962 at 971.

4 *Report of the Committee on Privacy and Related Matters*, Cm. 1102, Calcutt Committee, David Calcutt, chairman (1997).

5 "Australian Privacy Charter," Australian Privacy Foundation, www.privacy.org.au/About/ PrivacyCharter.html.

6 David Banisar and Simon Davies, "Global Trends in Privacy Protection: An International Survey of Privacy, Data Protection, and Surveillance Laws and Developments," *John Marshall Journal of Computer & Information Law* 18 (Fall 1999).

7   *Colloquium on Privacy & Security*, transcript, Gary M. Schober, moderator, *Buffalo L. Rev.* 50 (2002): 703, 726; *Privacy and Human Rights: An International Survey of Privacy Laws and Developments*, Electronic Privacy Information Center & Privacy International, 2002.

8   *Privacy and Human Rights*, 5.

9   an-Noor 24:27–28 (Yusufali); al-Hujraat 49:11–12 (Yusufali).

10 www.legislation.gov.uk/aep/Edw3/34/1.

11 *Entick v Carrington* [1765] EWHC KB J98, www.bailii.org/ew/cases/EWHC/KB/1765/J98.html.

12 William Pitt, Speech on the Excise Bill, House of Commons (March 1763).

13 Judgment of June 16, 1858, Trib. pr. inst. de la Seine, 1858 D.P. III 62 (Fr.) (affaire Rachel); see also Jeanne M. Hauch, "Protecting Private Facts in France: The Warren & Brandeis Tort Is Alive and Well and Flourishing in Paris," *Tul. L. Rev.* 68 (1994): 1219.

14 See *Norway—Privacy Profile*, Privacy International, 2011, https://www.privacyinternational.org/article/norway-privacy-profile.

15 Fiftieth Anniversary of the Universal Declaration of Human Rights, United Nations, www.un.org/rights/50/decla.htm.

16 *Id*. at Article 8.

17 American Declaration of the Rights and Duties of Man, April 1948, Conference of American States, www.cidh.oas.org/Basicos/English/Basic2.American%20Declaration.htm.

18 *Id*. at Article V.

19 Convention for the Protection of Human Rights and Fundamental Freedoms, April 11, 1950, Council of Europe, http://conventions.coe.int/treaty/en/treaties/html/005.htm.

20 *Id*. at Article 8.

21 Directive 95/46/EC of the European Parliament and of the Council of 24 October 1995 on the protection of individuals with regard to the processing of personal data and on the free movement of such data.

22 The types of data elements commonly found on a business card are excluded from coverage by the act.

23 Implementing guidelines are issued by the Ministry of Economy, Trade and Industry, the Ministry of Health, Labor and Welfare, the Financial Services Agency, the Ministry of Finance, the Ministry of Internal Affairs and Communications, the Ministry of Land, Infrastructure and Transport, and the Ministry of Justice.

24 http://eur-lex.europa.eu/LexUriServ/LexUriServ.do?uri=CELEX:31995L0046:EN:HTML.

25 http://laws-lois.justice.gc.ca/eng/acts/P-8.6/page-18.html#h-25.

26 Opinion 4/2007 on the concept of personal data, http://ec.europa.eu/justice/policies/privacy/docs/wpdocs/2007/wp136_en.pdf.

27 *EMI Records & Ors -v- Eircom Ltd.*, www.courts.ie/Judgments.nsf/09859e7a3f34669680256ef3004a27de/7e52f4a2660d8840802577070035082f?OpenDocument.

28 Office of Management and Budget, OMB Memorandum 07-16, "Safeguarding Against and Responding to the Breach of Personally Identifiable Information," www.whitehouse.gov/omb/memoranda/fy2007/m07-16.pdf.

29 Federal Register, FTC 16 CFR Part 318 Health Breach Notification Rule; Final Rule, www.ftc.gov/os/2009/08/R911002hbn.pdf.

30 Data Protection Directive at Article 2(d).

31 Federal Trade Commission, "Protecting Consumer Privacy in an Era of Rapid Change: A Proposed Framework for Businesses and Policymakers," December 2010.

32 "Privacy by Design: The 7 Foundational Principles," Office of the Information and Privacy Commissioner of Ontario, rev. January 2011, www.privacybydesign.ca/content/uploads/2009/08/7foundational principles.pdf.

33 Article 20 of the EU Commission's Proposal for a Regulation of the European Parliament and of the Council on the protection of individuals with regard to the processing of personal data and on the free movement of such data.

34 FTC, "Protecting Consumer Privacy," 2.

35 *Id.*

36 U.S. Department of Health, Education and Welfare, "Records, Computers, and the Rights of Citizens: Report of the Secretary's Advisory Committee on Automated Personal Data Systems, Records, Computers, and the Rights of Citizens," July 1973, viii.

37 *Guidelines Governing the Protection of Privacy and Transborder Data Flows of Personal Data*, Sept. 23, 1980, Organisation for Economic Co-operation and Development. An important distinction between the OECD and the COE is the involvement and support of the United States government. For more information, see www.oecd.org/document/18/0,3343,en_2649_34255_1815186_1_1_1_1,00.html.

38 Jordan M. Blanke, "'Safe Harbor' and the European Union's Directive on Data Protection," *Albany Law Journal of Science & Technology* (2000).

39 Convention for the Protection of Individuals with Regard to the Automatic Processing of Personal Data, Jan. 8, 1981, Council of Europe, http://conventions.coe.int/Treaty/en/Treaties/Html/108.htm.

40 Banisar and Davies, "Global Trends," 11. See also Jeffrey B. Ritter, Benjamin S. Hayes and Henry L. Judy, "Emerging Trends in International Privacy Law," *Emory International Law Review*, Spring 2001.

41 Ritter, Hayes and Judy, "Emerging Trends," 92.

42 *Id.*

43 www.apec.org/Groups/Committee-on-Trade-and-Investment/~/media/Files/Groups/ECSG/05_ecsg_ privacyframewk.ashx.

44 www.privacyconference2009.org/dpas_space/space_reserved/documentos_adoptados/common/2009 _Madrid/estandares_resolucion_madrid_en.pdf.

45 Bundesdatenschutzgesetz (BDSG), Federal Data Protection Act 1991, Council of Europe Doc. CJ-PD §36 (91) 30 (July 12, 1991).

46 This list of functions is based on the Nymity Data Privacy Reporting Model, January 2012, available upon request from Nymity Inc., www.nymity.com.

CHAPTER TWO

Geography

*Privacy and Data Protection Regulation
Around the World*

This chapter provides the foundation for understanding how privacy and data protection operate around the world. It begins by examining the complementary sources of privacy protection: markets, technology, law and self-regulation (or co-regulation). It then outlines key models of privacy protection: the comprehensive, sectoral, self-regulatory or co-regulatory, and technology models.

To deepen the understanding of these models, four examples are explored in depth:

- Comprehensive model, in the European Union

- Sectoral model, in the United States

- Co-regulatory model, in Australia

- No general privacy or data protection law, in the People's Republic of China

The chapter concludes with a review of the principal privacy and data protection laws in other countries, grouped by geographic area.

1. Sources of Privacy Protection

There is no single approach to protecting privacy and security. Rather, privacy protection is derived from several sources: market forces, technology, legal controls and self-regulation.

- **Markets.** The market can be a useful way of approaching privacy protection. When consumers raise concerns about their privacy, companies respond. Businesses that are brand sensitive are especially likely to adopt strict privacy practices, to build up their reputation as a trustworthy organization. In turn, this can create market competition, spurring other companies to also implement privacy practices into their operations.

- **Technology.** Technology also can provide robust privacy protection. The rapid advancement of technology provides people with new and advanced means of protecting themselves. Even if privacy protection from law or market forces is weak, information privacy and security best practices can remain strong.

- **Law.** Law is the traditional approach to privacy regulation. However, simply enacting more laws does not necessarily result in better privacy and security. Laws may not be well drafted and may be poorly enforced. Laws should be understood as one very important source of privacy protections, but in practice actual protection also depends on markets, technology and self-regulation.

- **Self-regulation/co-regulation.** Self-regulation (and the closely related concept of co-regulation) is a complement to law that comes from the government. The term *self-regulation* can refer to any or all of three components: legislation, enforcement and adjudication. Legislation refers to the question of who defines privacy rules. For self-regulation, this typically occurs through the privacy policy of a company or other entity, or by an industry association. Enforcement refers to the question of who should initiate enforcement action. Actions may be brought by data protection authorities, other government agencies, industry code enforcement or in some cases the affected individuals. Finally, adjudication refers to the question of who should decide whether an organization has violated a privacy rule. The decision maker can be an industry association, a government agency or a judicial officer; thus the term *self-regulation* covers a broad range of institutional arrangements. For a clear understanding of data privacy responsibilities, privacy professionals should consider who defines the requirements, which organization brings enforcement action and who actually makes the judicial decisions.

2. World Models of Data Protection

As of November 2011, according to one study, more than 80 countries had known data protection regimes, over half of which first enacted privacy laws after the year 2000.[1] The different data protection models around the world all draw upon law, markets, technology and self-regulation as sources for privacy protection in varying degrees. Comprehensive data protection laws are those in which the government has defined requirements throughout the economy. On the other hand, sectoral laws, such as those in the United States, exist in selected market segments, often in response to a particular need or problem. The scope of data protection laws, as described above, varies depending on how much the specific country relies on government laws versus industry codes and standards. The various data protection models used globally also differ in enforcement and adjudication. However, each regime falls along a continuum, with clearly defined legislative, enforcement and adjudication mechanisms established by the government at one end, and no stated, defined baseline at the other. In practice, no regime is so comprehensive that all laws are written, enforced and adjudicated by the government. However, even in the United States, which is often used as an example of a less regulatory-oriented regime, the government has written numerous privacy laws.

Some of the most common data protection models in use today are comprehensive and sectoral frameworks, the co-regulatory or self-regulatory models, and the technology-based model. Following are the basic approaches, along with major arguments for and against each approach.

2.1 Comprehensive Model

Comprehensive data protection laws govern the collection, use and dissemination of personal information in the public and private sectors.[2] Generally speaking, a country that has enacted such laws hosts an official or agency responsible for overseeing enforcement.[3] This official or agency, often referred to as a data protection authority (DPA), ensures compliance with the law and investigates alleged breaches of the law's provisions. In many countries, the official also bears the responsibility for educating the public on data protection matters and acts as an international liaison for data protection issues. Enforcement and funding are two critical issues in a comprehensive data protection scheme. Data protection officials are granted varying degrees of enforcement power from country to country. Further, countries choose to allocate varying levels of resources to the enforcement of data protection laws, leaving some countries inadequately funded to meet the laws' stated goals.

Countries over time have adopted comprehensive privacy and data protection laws for a combination of at least three reasons:[4]

1. **Remedy past injustices.** A number of countries, particularly those previously subject to authoritarian regimes, have enacted comprehensive laws as a means to remedy past privacy violations. For instance, Germany is widely regarded as having one of the strictest privacy regimes. At least part of the reason is likely a reaction to its history of the Nazi regime and to heavy surveillance by the Stasi (Ministry of State Security) in East Germany before the two parts of Germany were reunified in 1990.

2. **Ensure consistency with European privacy laws.** As discussed below, the Data Protection Directive in the European Union limits transfer of personal data to countries that lack "adequate" privacy protections. Nonmembers of the EU, such as in central and eastern Europe, have passed privacy laws as part of the process of joining the EU. Other countries have enacted privacy laws at least in part to prevent any disruption in trade with EU countries.

3. **Promote electronic commerce.** Countries have developed privacy laws to provide assurance to potentially uneasy consumers engaged in electronic commerce.

Critics of the comprehensive approach express concern that the costs of the regulations can outweigh the benefits. One-size-fits-all rules may not address risk well: If the rules are strict enough to assure protection for especially sensitive data, such as medical data or information that can lead to identity theft, that same level of strictness may not be justified for less sensitive data. Along with the strictness of controls, comprehensive regimes can have costly paperwork, documentation, audit and similar requirements even for settings where the risks are low.

A different critique of comprehensive regimes is that they may provide insufficient opportunity for innovation in data processing. With the continued evolution of computers, individuals have access today to many products and services that were unimaginable a decade or two ago, from smartphones to social networks to the full range of services that have developed since the Internet emerged in the 1990s. To the extent that comprehensive laws may discourage the emergence of new services involving personal information or require prior approval from regulators, the pace and diversity of technological innovation may slow.

2.2 Sectoral Model (United States, Japan)

This framework protects personal information by enacting laws that address a particular industry sector.[5] For example, in the United States different laws delineate conduct and specify the requisite level of data protection for video rental records, consumer financial transactions, credit records, law enforcement and medical records. In a comprehensive model, laws addressing specific market segments may be enacted to provide more specific protection for data particular to that segment, such as the healthcare sector.

Supporters of the sectoral approach emphasize that different parts of the economy face different privacy and security challenges; it is appropriate, for instance, to have stricter regulation for medical records than for ordinary commerce. Supporters also underscore the cost savings and lack of regulatory burden for organizations outside of the regulated sectors.

Critics of the sectoral approach express concern about the lack of a single data protection authority to oversee personal information issues. They also point out the problems of gaps and overlaps in coverage. Gaps can occur when legislation lags behind technological change, and unregulated segments may suddenly face privacy threats with no legislative guidance. Whereas laws under the comprehensive approach apply to new technologies, there are no similar governmental rules under the sectoral approach until the legislature or other responsible body acts. Moreover, there can be political obstacles to creating new legislation if industry or other stakeholders oppose such laws. An example of a gap being filled is the Health Information Technology for Economic and Clinical Health (HITECH) Act of 2009, which introduced a breach notification requirement for personal health records vendors such as Google Health and Microsoft HealthVault. These were not "covered entities" under the Health Insurance Portability and Accountability Act (HIPAA). The new law addressed a gap, where entities not traditionally involved in healthcare offered services involving the collection and use of large volumes of healthcare information.

Similarly, overlaps can exist in a sectoral approach. For instance, HIPAA-covered entities such as medical providers are subject to enforcement either by the U.S. Department of Health and Human Services under HIPAA or by the Federal Trade Commission (FTC) under its general authority to take action against unfair and deceptive practices. As the boundaries between industries change over time, previously separate industries can converge, potentially leading to different legal treatment of functionally similar activities. In the United States, cable television and telephone providers have historically been regulated under separate laws, but both now provide Internet service to homes, as do other companies not under a regulatory law for personal information. The multiple legal rules thus can lead to complexity and compliance costs.

2.3 The Co-regulatory and Self-regulatory Models

Co-regulation and self-regulation are quite similar, with co-regulation generally referring to laws such as those in Australia, which are closer to the comprehensive model, and self-regulation generally referring to approaches such as in the United States or Singapore, where there are no general laws applying to personal information. Under both approaches, a mix of government and nongovernment institutions protect personal information.

The **co-regulatory model** emphasizes industry development of enforceable codes or standards for privacy and data protection, against the backdrop of legal requirements by the government. Co-regulation can exist under both comprehensive and sectoral models.

Co-regulation is a prominent feature of the law in Australia and New Zealand. These countries have a privacy or information commissioner with overarching responsibility for privacy and data protection issues. The national laws encourage creation of industry-specific codes, which, once promulgated, have effect in place of the underlying statutory protections.

As a variation on the comprehensive model, the Netherlands has extensive experience with codes developed in close consultation with industry, and breach of such codes is considered a violation of the Netherlands Data Protection Act. Similarly, Ireland gives force to such codes once approved by both the Data Protection Commissioner and Parliament.[6]

As a variation on the sectoral model, the Children's Online Privacy Protection Act in the United States allows compliance with codes to be sufficient for compliance with the statute once the codes have been approved by the FTC.

The **self-regulatory model** emphasizes creation of codes of practice for the protection of personal information by a company, industry or independent body. In contrast to the co-regulatory model, there may be no generally applicable data protection law that creates a legal framework for the self-regulatory code.[7]

The following are two examples of self-regulatory models that have global impact:

- The Payment Card Industry Data Security Standard was developed to encourage and enhance cardholder data security and facilitate the broad adoption of consistent data security measures globally.

- The Groupe Speciale Mobile Association has created a framework that identifies the privacy standards that mobile users can expect.[8]

Both of these self-regulatory models require all participating organizations to comply with the provisions of the code.

One early self-regulatory effort was the Online Privacy Alliance (OPA),[9] a coalition of prominent online companies and trade associations established in 1998 to encourage the self-regulation of online privacy.[10] Under these guidelines, OPA members agreed to post a privacy policy to inform users about how information about them was being collected and used. The guidelines did not themselves provide for enforcement but instead encouraged members to establish enforcement mechanisms independently.[11]

Seal programs are another form of self-regulation. A seal program requires its participants to abide by codes of information practices and submit to some variation of monitoring to ensure compliance.[12] Companies that abide by the terms of the seal program are then allowed to display the program's privacy seal on their website. Examples of such programs are TRUSTe, BBBOnline, WebTrust, EuroPriSe, the AMIPCI Trust Mark and TrustSG.[13]

Supporters of a self-regulatory approach tend to emphasize the expertise of the industry to inform its own personal information practices, and thus the most efficient ways to assure privacy and security. Self-regulatory codes may also be more flexible and quick to adjust to new technology, without the need for prior governmental approval.

Critics of the self-regulatory approach often express concerns about adequacy and enforcement. Industry-developed codes can provide limited data protection, and may not adequately incorporate the perspectives and interests of consumers and other stakeholders who are not part of the industry. The strength of enforcement can also vary. In some cases, where an organization has signed up for a code, any violation is treated the same as a violation of a statute. In others, however, penalties can be weak, and there may be no effective enforcement authority.

2.4 The Technology-Based Model

The technology-based model is useful to consider as an alternative to protections that arise from an organization's administrative compliance with laws or self-regulatory codes. Individuals and organizations in some settings can use technical measures that reduce the relative importance of administrative measures for overall privacy protection. For example, global web e-mail providers such as Google and Microsoft have been increasing their use of encryption between the sender and recipient. For securely encrypted e-mail, the local Internet service provider can no longer read the text of the communication. With this technical change, the personal information practices of the Internet service provider (ISP) thus become less relevant to protection of the content of the communication. Chapters 4 and 5 further discuss the interrelated roles of technical, administrative and physical safeguards for personal information.

3. Major Privacy and Data Protection Regimes

It is useful to consider examples of the major regulatory approaches for privacy and data protection (listed at the start of this chapter). After examining the laws under each model, the discussion will then review national data protection laws, organized by geographic region.

3.1 Comprehensive Model (European Union)

In 1995, the European Union passed Directive 95/46/EC on the protection of individuals with regard to the processing of personal data and on the free movement of such data (known more commonly as the **EU Data Protection Directive** or "the Directive"). This is the EU's comprehensive, overarching legal structure to protect the fundamental rights and freedoms of EU citizens, in particular the right to privacy with respect to the processing of personal data. The EU Data Protection Directive went into effect in 1998. A new regulation to revise and replace the Directive was proposed in 2012. The discussion here describes the Directive as promulgated in 1995.

3.1.1 Applicability

The Directive imposes strict requirements on any person who collects or processes data pertaining to individuals. The general rule is not to allow any collection or use of personal data unless permitted under law. The Directive is based on a set of data protection principles, which include legitimate basis for processing; purpose limitation; data quality; proportionality; transparency; data security and confidentiality; data subjects' rights of access, rectification, deletion and objection; restrictions on onward transfers; additional protection where special categories of data and direct marketing are involved; and a prohibition on automated individual decisions.

As noted, the Directive's scope is broad. It applies to all sectors of industry and to all types of personal data. The Directive's key provisions impose serious restrictions on personal data processing, grant individual rights to "data subjects," and set forth specific procedural obligations, including notification to national authorities. The 1995 Directive requires each member state to promulgate a national law, so some variations have existed to date in how its provisions are implemented.

3.1.2 Core Principles

Section I, Article 6 of the Directive codifies the fair information practices first developed in the United States in the 1970s, and states that EU member states shall provide that personal data must be:[14]

- Processed fairly and lawfully.

- Collected for specified, explicit and legitimate purposes and not further processed in a way incompatible with those purposes. Further processing of data for historical, statistical or scientific purposes shall not be considered as incompatible provided that member states provide appropriate safeguards.

- Adequate, relevant and not excessive in relation to the purposes for which they are collected and/or further processed.

- Accurate and, where necessary, kept up to date; every reasonable step must be taken to ensure that data which are inaccurate or incomplete, having regard to the purposes for which they were collected or for which they are further processed, are erased or rectified.

- Kept in a form which permits identification of data subjects for no longer than is necessary for the purposes for which the data were collected or for which they are further processed. Member states shall lay down appropriate safeguards for personal data stored for longer periods for historical, statistical or scientific use.

3.1.3 Data Processing

The Directive regulates the "processing" of "personal data." The term *personal data* is broadly defined as data that relates to an identified or identifiable individual, including (for example) business contact information and information about an individual acting in a business or professional capacity. Personal data obtained from public sources is also covered.

According to the Information Commissioner of the United Kingdom, for example, data is likely to be personal data when it:[15]

- Relates to the identifiable individual (whether in personal or family life, business or profession)
- Is obviously about the individual (for example, medical history, criminal record, personal bank statements, record of work, etc.)
- Is used to inform or influence actions or decisions affecting an identifiable individual (for example, data about an individual's phone or electricity account clearly determine what the individual will be charged)
- Is linked to an individual so that it provides particular information about that individual (for example, for a single named individual employed in a particular post, the salary information about the post is personal data)

The term *processing* is defined to cover all operations performed on "personal data," including collection, storage, handling, use and deletion. Both manual and automated processing activities are covered. To accommodate other important interests, the Directive provides for partial exemptions for certain activities, such as journalism and research, but only if such exemptions are necessary to reconcile the right to privacy with the rules governing the freedom of expression and if the member states provide "appropriate safeguards," such as an obligation to render personal data anonymous.

3.1.4 General Processing Prohibition and Exceptions

Personal data may be processed only in certain specific situations described in the Directive. For example, processing is permitted if the "unambiguous consent" (as discussed below) of the individual has been obtained.

Processing is also permitted if it is necessary for the performance of a contract to which the data subject is party. This scenario is particularly important in business-to-consumer transactions, such as to deliver a package to a home, although the exception is applied narrowly. For example, a contractual clause with a third party would not be covered, if it provides for processing of data other than that needed to service the customer.

Processing is also permitted when "necessary for the purposes of the legitimate interests" of the company or a third party or parties to whom data is disclosed, except where the business interests are overridden by the interests for fundamental rights and freedoms of the consumer. In this vaguely defined category of cases, processing is justified if there is an acceptable balance between the company's business interests and the consumer's interests. Unlike the situations described above, this ground requires that a balancing test be applied in each specific case.

3.1.5 International Data Transfers: "Adequacy," Model Contracts and Binding Corporate Rules

The Directive was enacted for dual purposes: to enhance the free flow of data among the EU member states while also providing for a high level of data protection.[16] The Directive is designed to ensure the free movement of data within Europe, consistent with the European Union's rules for a unified market, and European data protection laws do not impose data transfer restrictions on data flows within the EU, although registration and notification requirements still apply. However, the Directive strictly regulates transfers of personal data to non-EU countries. In particular, personal data may not be transferred to jurisdictions outside of the EU unless the jurisdictions offer an "adequate level of protection" for the data or another basis for the transfer exists.[17]

With regard to adequacy, the European Commission, as of early 2012, declared the following jurisdictions to offer adequate legal protection, so that data transfers can occur in these instances without further approvals or processes: Switzerland, Argentina, Guernsey, the Isle of Man, Jersey, Faroe Islands, Andorra, Israel and Canada, as long as the recipient of the information is subject to the Canadian Personal Information Protection and Electronic Documents Act (PIPEDA).[18]

Organizations seeking to transfer data to countries that have not been deemed adequate are encouraged to implement **model contracts**, which contain standard contractual clauses. Standard contractual clauses are agreements defined by the EU and the Article 29 Working Party for the purpose of meeting the adequacy standards defined under the Directive. Standard model clauses contain extensive data protection commitments and company liability requirements. Organizations must be willing to implement the standard contractual clauses for each business process or personal data flow originating from an EU country to a country that has not been deemed adequate. These contractual agreements help to ensure that an organization can avoid enforcement actions and interruptions in global business dealings.

Binding corporate rules (BCRs) are legally binding internal corporate privacy rules for transferring personal information within a corporate group, established by the EU Article 29 Working Party. BCRs are typically used by corporations that operate in different jurisdictions, and are alternatives to the U.S.-EU Safe Harbor and model contract clauses. Before BCRs become effective they must be approved by the EU data protection authorities of the different states in which the corporation operates.

A lead authority must be designated as the point of contact. This authority handles the procedure for review of the BCR and coordinates the authorization process from other data protection authorities in all European jurisdictions in which that company operates. The decision on who shall be the lead authority should be based on the location:

- of the group's European headquarters;
- of the company within the group that has delegated data protection responsibilities;
- of the company within the group best placed to deal with the application and enforce the BCRs;
- where most decisions are taken in relation to the processing; and
- where the most transfers outside the EU take place.

The finalization of the draft BCR generally requires exchanges between the company and the lead DPA. If satisfied, the lead DPA forwards them to two other designated authorities, who have one month to review and submit their comments. At the end of that process the lead authority sends the draft BCR to all DPAs in the countries from which the data is transferred.[19]

3.1.6. The EU e-Privacy Directive (2002/58/EC)

As electronic commerce has developed, the European Commission has issued various directives to address different types of technology and business practices (such as the adoption of distance contracts). Many of these directives address privacy implications of the technology or practice. For example, in 1997, the Telecommunications Directive was promulgated to address the use of telephonic marketing (phone and fax) by means of automated calling systems and predictive dialers.[20] This directive prohibited the use of these technologies unless express (opt-in) consent of the individuals had been obtained.[21]

In 2002, given concerns about the rise of unsolicited commercial e-mail, the European Commission revised, renamed and reenacted the Telecommunications Directive as the e-Privacy Directive so that it could better address the range of issues related to electronic communications.[22]

Known formally as the directive on privacy and electronic communications (2002/58/ EC), the e-Privacy Directive was adopted with the purpose of regulating the privacy and data protection issues inherent in online marketing practices. It extends controls on unsolicited direct marketing to all forms of electronic communications, including unsolicited commercial e-mail and short message service (SMS—i.e., text messages) to mobile telephones. Following are some of the key provisions of the 2002 directive:

- Individuals must give prior opt-in consent before receiving e-mail. However, if there is an existing customer relationship, companies may e-mail (or text) such customers provided that they are marketing their own similar products and the customer is easily able to opt out of receiving such communications in the future.

- "Cookie" files and similar online identification mechanisms are required to be more transparent, and anyone using them must provide information about them to subscribers or users and offer an opportunity to refuse them.

- Individual subscribers have stronger rights to decide whether or not they want to be listed in subscriber directories. Subscribers must be given clear information about the directories and must be informed of any reverse search.

- Value-added services (e.g., location-based advertising to mobile phones) are permitted, so long as subscribers have given their consent and are informed of the data processing implications.

- The directive gives member states the authority to introduce provisions on the retention of traffic and location data for law enforcement purposes.

In 2009, the European Parliament made additions to the e-Privacy Directive (Directive 2009/136/EC, also known as the EU Cookie Directive). According to the 2002 version, websites could allow consumers to opt out of cookies, such as by selecting a setting on their web browsers. Under the revision, member states are required to pass legislation that gives users the right to opt in before cookies are placed on their computers. The initial deadlines for implementing the Cookie Directive were not met by the majority of member states, due in part to an ongoing process of clarification about what categories of cookies are not covered (such as to enable basic website functioning) and how in a practical way to provide opt-in consent for cookies.

3.1.7 The Article 29 Working Party

The Data Protection Directive that went into effect in 1998 formed the **Article 29 Working Party**, a group of data protection authorities that has provided guidance on a wide range of data protection issues.[23] The laws are actually enforced by the national DPAs of EU member states as well as the data protection authority of the European Commission itself.

3.1.8 Employment Data

The EU emphasizes employee rights in the protection of employment data held by an organization. To a greater extent than in the United States, privacy concerns tend to predominate over security concerns, and employee monitoring is permitted only with specific, legal justification. Background checks of employees are limited and employees have broad privacy expectations and rights. Also, employers are often required to consult with regulatory bodies and comply with contracts, including trade union and works council agreements, which place limits on employer processing of employee information.

3.1.9 The EU-U.S. Safe Harbor Agreement

The Directive generally forbids transfer of personal data to countries that lack "adequate" data protection, and the EU to date has not found "adequate" protection in the United States. To navigate around this impediment, the U.S. Department of Commerce, in consultation with the European Commission, developed a "Safe Harbor" framework.

Corporations that agree to participate in the Safe Harbor promise to apply fair information practices, as set forth in the Safe Harbor framework. These promises apply to personal data that is transferred from the EU to the United States. Companies that implement a Safe Harbor privacy program annually certify their compliance with the Department of Commerce. For enforcement, corporations subject themselves to the authority and jurisdiction of a U.S. enforcement authority. Currently two U.S. regulatory agencies, the FTC and the Department of Transportation (DOT), have agreed to enforce Safe Harbor violations.[24] The FTC considers it an unfair and deceptive trade practice subject to enforcement if a corporation promises to abide by the Safe Harbor principles but fails to do so.

The following seven Safe Harbor requirements are, in large part, based on commonly established fair information practices:[25]

1. **Notice.** *Organizations must notify individuals about the purposes for which they collect and use information about them. They must provide information about how individuals can contact the organization with any inquiries or complaints, the types of third parties to which they disclose the information and the choices and means the organization offers for limiting its use and disclosure.*

2. **Choice.** *Organizations must give individuals the opportunity to choose (opt out) whether their personal information will be disclosed to a third party or used for a purpose incompatible with the purpose for which it was originally collected or subsequently authorized by the individual. For sensitive information, affirmative or explicit (opt in)* *choice must be given if the information is to be disclosed to a third party or used for a purpose other than its original purpose or the purpose authorized subsequently by the individual.*

*3. **Onward transfer (transfers to third parties).** To disclose information to a third party, organizations must apply the notice and choice principles. Where an organization wishes to transfer information to a third party that is acting as an agent, it may do so if it makes sure that the third party subscribes to the Safe Harbor principles or is subject to the Directive or another adequacy finding. As an alternative, the organization can enter into a written agreement with such third party requiring that the third party provide at least the same level of privacy protection as required by the relevant principles.*

*4. **Access.** Individuals must have access to personal information about them that an organization holds and be able to correct, amend, or delete that information where it is inaccurate, except where the burden or expense of providing access would be disproportionate to the risks to the individual's privacy in the case in question, or where the rights of persons other than the individual would be violated.*

*5. **Security.** Organizations must take reasonable precautions to protect personal information from loss, misuse and unauthorized access, disclosure, alteration and destruction.*

*6. **Data integrity.** Personal information must be relevant for the purposes for which it is to be used. An organization should take reasonable steps to ensure that data are reliable for their intended use, accurate, complete, and current.*

*7. **Enforcement.** In order to ensure compliance with the Safe Harbor principles, there must be (a) readily available and affordable independent recourse mechanisms so that each individual's complaints and disputes can be investigated and resolved and damages awarded where the applicable law or private sector initiatives so provide; (b) procedures for verifying that the commitments companies make to adhere to the Safe Harbor principles have been implemented; and (c) obligations to remedy problems arising out of a failure to comply with the principles. Sanctions must be sufficiently rigorous to ensure compliance by the organization. Organizations that fail to provide annual self-certification letters will no longer appear in the list of participants and Safe Harbor benefits will no longer be assured.*

Significantly, participation in the Safe Harbor program is not available to financial institutions and others that are not regulated by the U.S. FTC or DOT.

Alternatives to Safe Harbor. Companies seeking to provide adequate protection for EU purposes, but not wanting to go through Safe Harbor certification, may agree to abide by contracts approved by a relevant EU DPA, including the model contracts, discussed above.[26] Consent (or any other exception under the Directive) is another alternative to Safe Harbor. Data transfers can generally be authorized by consent. Such consent must be freely given and unambiguous, but the details of what constitutes consent vary among EU member states. Individuals must be able to withhold or revoke consent with no adverse consequences. EU authorities do not always recognize consent for human resources data because of the subordinate nature of the employer-employee relationship. A similar Safe Harbor agreement exists for personal data transferred from Switzerland to the United States.[27]

3.2. The Sectoral Model: The United States

The United States approach to privacy protection is quite different from the comprehensive legislation that countries have enacted under the EU Data Protection Directive. Instead of having one systematic source of legal authority, U.S. privacy protections have grown piecemeal over time. It is often said that the United States has a "sectoral" approach to privacy protection because different economic sectors, such as healthcare and financial services, operate under different legal requirements. As discussed above, self-regulation often applies for sectors that are not subject to specific statutes.

In contrast to European legal texts that define privacy with respect to the processing of personal information as a human right, the U.S. Constitution does not explicitly provide a right to privacy.[28] Legal attention to the "right to privacy" first became prominent in 1890, when concerns about the growth of photography in the press led Brandeis and Warren to declare that privacy was the right to be free from intrusion, "the right to be left alone."[29] Seventy years later, the legal scholar William Prosser elaborated on these principles in a law review article[30] setting forth a number of privacy torts, such as for public revelation of private facts.[31] Over time, courts have announced a series of privacy rights based on the Constitution, granting individual rights over personal matters such as birth control,[32] abortion,[33] and sexual activities.[34] These rights are about "decisional" privacy, however, and not the "information" privacy that is the focus of this book. For information privacy, statutes rather than constitutional law provide the primary source of legal obligations.

Two approaches to privacy legislation are prominent today in the United States. One is the fair information practices discussed in Chapter 1. Key principles include notice and choice. This approach emphasizes processes for collection and use of personal information and is exemplified by the Financial Services Modernization Act of 1999, usually referred to as the Gramm-Leach-Bliley Act in honor of its main legislative authors.[35] The second is the "permissible purpose" approach, which limits data usage to purposes permitted under the law. The Fair Credit Reporting Act is the best example of this approach.[36] Some privacy laws—such as the medical privacy rule under the HIPAA of 1996—include both process elements and permissible uses.

The Code of Fair Information Practices (also known as the Code of Fair Information Principles) was first developed in the early 1970s by the U.S. Department of Health, Education and Welfare Advisory Committee on Automated Data Systems.[37] Variations on this code were issued over time. In 2012, the Obama administration announced a "Consumer Privacy Bill of Rights" as an updated set of Fair Information Practice Principles.[38] Although this Consumer Privacy Bill of Rights has not been enacted into law, in the view of the U.S. government under

President Obama, the following principles should apply to personal information in modern online commercial settings:

1. **Individual control.** Consumers have a right to exercise control over what personal data companies collect from them and how they use it.

2. **Transparency.** Consumers have a right to easily understandable and accessible information about privacy and security practices.

3. **Respect for context.** Consumers have a right to expect that companies will collect, use and disclose personal data in ways that are consistent with the context in which consumers provide the data.

4. **Security.** Consumers have a right to secure and responsible handling of personal data.

5. **Access and accuracy.** Consumers have a right to access and correct personal data in usable formats, in a manner that is appropriate to the sensitivity of the data and the risk of adverse consequences to consumers if the data is inaccurate.

6. **Focused collection.** Consumers have a right to reasonable limits on the personal data that companies collect and retain.

7. **Accountability.** Consumers have a right to have personal data handled by companies with appropriate measures in place to assure they adhere to the Consumer Privacy Bill of Rights.

3.2.1. Federal Privacy Laws

A few key U.S. federal privacy laws are profiled here, providing examples of privacy laws and regulations within the U.S. private sector (concerning for-profit, commercial organizations) and the U.S. public sector (concerning government agencies).

Key private sector privacy laws include:

- **Fair Credit Reporting Act (FCRA).** The FCRA was enacted in 1970 to mandate accurate and relevant data collection, to give consumers the ability to access and correct their information, and to limit the use of consumer reports to permissible purposes, such as employment and extension of credit or insurance.[39]

- **Health Insurance Portability and Accountability Act of 1996 (HIPAA).** HIPAA was enacted by Congress, among other purposes, to create national standards for electronic healthcare transactions. Congress recognized, however, that the movement to electronic data exchange in the healthcare sector posed risks to privacy and security. Accordingly, HIPAA required the U.S. Department of Health and Human Services to promulgate comprehensive regulations to protect the privacy and security of personal health information. The basic rule is that patients have to opt in before their information can be shared with other organizations, although there are important exceptions such as for treatment, payment and healthcare operations. Congress amended important parts of HIPAA in the HITECH Act of 2009.

- **Gramm-Leach-Bliley Act (GLBA).** The Financial Services Modernization Act of 1999, known as the Gramm-Leach-Bliley Act, reorganized financial services regulation in the United States.[40] GLBA applies broadly to financial institutions (i.e., any company that is "significantly engaged" in financial activities in the United States). In its privacy provisions, GLBA addresses the handling of nonpublic personal information, defined broadly to include a consumer's name and address, and consumers' interactions with banks, insurers and other financial institutions. Enforcement is done by financial regulators and the Consumer Financial Protection Bureau. GLBA's basic requirements are to:
  - Securely store personal financial information
  - Give notice of policies regarding the sharing of personal financial information
  - Give consumers the ability to opt out of some sharing of personal financial information
- **Children's Online Privacy Protection Act of 1998 (COPPA).** COPPA applies to the operators of commercial websites and online services that are directed to children under the age of 13.[41] It also applies to general audience websites and online services that have actual knowledge that they are collecting personal information from children under the age of 13. COPPA requires these website operators to post a privacy policy on the homepage of the website; provide notice about collection practices to parents; obtain verifiable parental consent before collecting personal information from children; give parents a choice as to whether their child's personal information will be disclosed to third parties; provide parents access and the opportunity to delete the child's personal information and opt out of future collection or use of the information; and maintain the confidentiality, security and integrity of personal information collected from children.

Along with these sectoral laws, the FTC has authority under Section 5 of the Federal Trade Commission Act to bring enforcement actions against "unfair and deceptive" trade practices. The FTC jurisdiction extends broadly to commercial entities, with exceptions for the financial services and certain other sectors. Many of the FTC's privacy enforcement actions have been for "deceptive" trade practices, when a company has failed to comply with commitments it has made in its privacy policies. The U.S. Congress has passed specific laws for protection of personal information in additional sectors such as cable television, education, telecommunications customer information and video rentals. In addition, U.S. legislation exists for specific marketing activities, such as telemarketing, junk faxes and unsolicited commercial e-mail.

Key public sector privacy laws include:

- **The Privacy Act of 1974.** This legislation was passed in response to the executive branch's less-than-scrupulous data-gathering practices in the late 1960s and 1970s. The act regulates the federal government's use of computerized databases of information about U.S. citizens and permanent, legal residents. It also establishes fair information practices that each agency must follow when collecting, using or disclosing personal information, including rights of citizen action and redress for violations.

- **The Freedom of Information Act (FOIA).** This law was enacted in 1966 to ensure citizen access to federal government agency records.[42] FOIA covers all federal agency records, not just those that contain personal information. FOIA applies only to federal executive branch documents—it does not apply to legislative (congressional) or judicial records. It also does not apply to state or local records, although nearly all state governments have their own FOIA-type statutes.[43] For federal agencies, FOIA provides access to all federal agency records, subject to nine specific exemptions. The federal and most state FOIA statutes include a specific exemption for personal information, so that sensitive data (such as Social Security numbers) is not disclosed inadvertently during the open government process. FOIA was updated to apply broadly to electronic records in the Electronic Freedom of Information Act of 1996 (E-FOIA).[44]

3.2.2 State Privacy Laws

Legal compliance in the United States depends both on federal law, discussed above, and on any applicable state law. Nearly all of the 50 states now have some sort of data breach notification law in place, although details vary. States have numerous other privacy laws, including legislation on topics such as identity theft and medical privacy. Some federal privacy statutes, such as the FCRA, preempt state law, so that states cannot make additional requirements. Others, such as HIPAA, do not preempt state law, and stricter privacy protections can thus be added at the state level. Among the states, California is often viewed as the leading legislator, and its large population and high-tech sector mean that the requirements of California law receive particular attention.

3.3 The Co-Regulatory Model: Australia

Australia has a co-regulatory approach to information privacy. Australia's Federal Privacy Act contains 11 information privacy principles that apply to Commonwealth and ACT (Australian Capital Territory) government agencies.[45] Amendments to this act have extended the country's existing National Privacy Principles into the private sector. The Privacy Amendment (Private Sector) Act 2000 now regulates how businesses collect, use and store personal information across the country.[46] The 10 National Privacy Principles apply to parts of the private sector and all health service providers as well as private sector data-processing activities.[47] These principles dictate that:

1. Collection must be fair and lawful.
2. Use and disclosure of data must occur only with consent.
3. Reasonable data quality and accuracy must be maintained.
4. Reasonable security must be maintained.
5. Openness (publication of organization's privacy policies) must be fulfilled.
6. A means for access and correction must be provided.

7. Use of government-issued identifiers must be limited.

8. Reasonable anonymity options must be offered.

9. Trans-border data flows should be limited.

10. Special protection must be implemented for sensitive data.

The Australian National Privacy Commissioner has some regulatory functions under other enactments, including the Telecommunications Act 1997, National Health Act 1953, Data Matching Program Act of 1990 and the Crimes Act of 1914.

Instead of defining specific procedures and standards within the national law, Australia has encouraged industry organizations to develop self-regulatory codes that reflect the National Privacy Principles. The Australian National Privacy Commissioner assists with code development, approves the codes and provides an independent enforcement mechanism for resolving complaints.

Additionally, instead of strict standards, the Australian law generally ties the obligations of an organization to what is "reasonable" for the organization under the circumstances. Data subjects do not have absolute rights under the Australian law. This hybrid regulatory/self-regulatory approach and the focus on "reasonableness" reflect the Australian government's attempt to provide adequate privacy protection within a business-facilitating framework.

3.4. No General Privacy or Data Protection Laws: People's Republic of China

The People's Republic of China (PRC) has not enacted a comprehensive privacy or data protection law. Indeed, some scholars have discussed the possibility of different cultural values with respect to privacy. In China, it is unclear how the traditional Chinese emphasis on the community will be reconciled over time with the individual rights approach emphasized by data protection law.

The Constitution of the PRC establishes an individual right to privacy. Article 40 of the Constitution protects an individual's freedom and privacy of communications.[48] Article 38 of the Constitution provides a basic right of individuals to be free from infringements on dignity and offers protection against defamation, false accusations and insults.[49] Little guidance has been provided that explains what constitutes illegal data processing, collection and use.

In early 2011, the General Administration of Quality Supervision Inspection and Quarantine and the Standardization Administration of the PRC published draft privacy guidelines entitled "Information Security Technology—Guide of Personal Information Protection."[50] If enacted, the guidelines would establish broad privacy rules for the collection, use and handling of personal information.

4. Privacy and Data Protection Regimes Grouped by Geographic Area

The preceding sections explained the basic models for privacy and data protection laws; the next sections review national laws, grouped by geographic region: Europe outside of the EU, the Americas outside of the United States, Asia/Pacific outside of Australia, the Middle East and Africa. In the past decade, there has been a large increase in the number of countries that have issued privacy and data protection laws that are broad in scope. This trend toward adoption is likely to continue in other countries, so privacy professionals should be alert to the possibility of new laws coming into effect. In countries with these nascent laws, however, government staff and enforcement are often not at the same level as in countries that have enforced privacy and data protection laws for a greater period of time.

4.1 Europe Outside of the European Union

European law is based on the protection of privacy as a fundamental human right. The general approach is to promulgate a comprehensive data protection regime and not allow any collection or use of personal data unless permitted under law.

As of 2012, the Data Protection Directive applied within the European Economic Area (EEA), consisting of 27 EU member states and the three European Free Trade Association (EFTA) countries that have signed onto the EEA agreement.

The 27 member states are Austria, Belgium, Bulgaria, Cyprus, the Czech Republic, Denmark, Estonia, Finland, France, Germany, Greece, Hungary, Ireland, Italy, Latvia, Lithuania, Luxembourg, Malta, the Netherlands, Poland, Portugal, Romania, Slovakia, Slovenia, Spain, Sweden and the United Kingdom. Additional candidates as of 2012 include Croatia, Iceland, the former Yugoslav Republic of Macedonia, Montenegro and Turkey.

The three EFTA countries that follow the Directive are Iceland, Liechtenstein and Norway. Switzerland is an EFTA member but not an EEA member and is therefore not required to comply with the Directive. Its national law, however, is very similar to the Directive.

4.1.1 European Countries Outside of the EEA with Data Protection Laws

4.1.1.1 Andorra

The Qualified Law 15/2003 regulates the protection of personal data; it incorporates the data protection principles of purpose limitation, data quality, proportionality, transparency, security and the right of data subjects to access, rectification and opposition. The law aims to regulate the treatment of data by both private entities and the Andorran public administration.

4.1.1.2 Armenia

The Law of the Republic of Armenia on Personal Data has been in force since 2003. The law applies to the public and private sectors and contains regulations for maintaining databases and notice and consent requirements.

4.1.1.3 Azerbaijan

The Law of the Republic of Azerbaijan on Information, Information Provision and Protection of Information, which came into force in 1998, applies to the public and private sectors. The law defines state policy on information systems, types, ways and forms of collecting and use of information data.

4.1.1.4 Bosnia and Herzegovina

The Law on the Protection of Personal Data applies to public bodies at the level of Bosnia and Herzegovina and to both public and private bodies of the Federation of Bosnia and Herzegovina and Republika Srpska and the District of Brcko of Bosnia and Herzegovina. The law recognizes basic principles of data protection including legitimacy, proportionality, transparency, purpose limitation and rights of access, rectification and deletion.

4.1.1.5 Belarus

The Law on Information, Informatization, and Protection of Information of November 10, 2008, establishes a nonexhaustive list of data considered to be personal, including family privacy, privacy of communications and health data. The collection, storage and processing of personal data are allowed only upon consent of the individual, and data holders must ensure the security of the information.

4.1.1.6 Croatia

The Personal Data Protection Act came into effect in 2003 and regulates the processing of personal data by government bodies and by legal and natural persons. The law implements principles similar to those in the EU Directive including prior consent for processing, purpose specification, data minimization and data accuracy.

4.1.1.7 Kosovo

The Law on the Protection of Personal Data was promulgated by decree of the president on May 13, 2010, and determines the rights, responsibilities, principles and measures with respect to personal data, which is information identifiable to a natural person by reference to an identification number or a physical, physiological, mental, economic, cultural or social identity. Personal data must be processed in a manner that complies with the purpose specification, accuracy and limited retention principles.

4.1.1.8 Moldova

The Law Nr. 17-XVI of 15.02.2007 on personal data protection applies to the processing of personal data. The law includes basic conditions of personal data processing and addresses lawful processing, proportionality, purpose limitation and rights of the data subject.

4.1.1.9 Russia

The Federal Law of 27 July 2006 N 152-FZ on Personal Data is similar in its approach to the EU Directive. It regulates activities related to the processing of personal data by federal, regional and other state agencies, municipal and other local authorities, legal entities and individuals. The law was amended and came into force on July 27, 2011, and includes amendments to privacy provisions (e.g., individuals may now consent to processing of their personal data through a representative) and security provisions (e.g., requiring security risk assessments and access controls).

4.1.1.10 Serbia

The Law on Personal Data Protection (published in the Official Gazette of the Republic of Serbia No. 97/08) applies to processing carried out by government organizations and personal data filing system controllers. The law governs the conditions for collection and processing of personal data, the rights of data subjects and the protection of those rights, and limitations to data protection.

4.1.1.11 Ukraine

Law No. 2297-VI on Personal Data Protection came into effect on January 1, 2011, and provides a general data protection framework for personal database owners, who have the right to process personal data according to law or the consent of the data subject.

4.2 The Americas Outside of the United States

4.2.1 Canada

Despite its geographic proximity to the United States, Canada is closer in philosophy and approach to the European model of data protection. Information privacy matters are managed by the industries concerned as well as overseen by the Canadian federal, provincial and territorial data protection commissioners (known as "information and privacy commissioners" and in some cases as "ombudsmen"). These Canadian government officials hold broad oversight powers and enforcement abilities but as of 2011 do not rely on fines.

4.2.1.1 The Privacy Act of 1983

The Privacy Act of 1983 provides rules and obligations on federal government departments and agencies to limit the collection, use and disclosure of personal information.[51] It also provides individuals with the right to access and correct personal information under the control of the government.

4.2.1.2 The Personal Information Protection and Electronic Documents Act of 2000 (PIPEDA)

PIPEDA is Canada's comprehensive national private sector privacy legislation.[52] The act became fully applicable to all industry segments in 2004 and has two goals: (1) to instill trust in electronic commerce and private sector transactions for Canadian citizens and (2) to establish a level playing field where the same marketplace rules apply to all businesses.

PIPEDA applies to "every organization" with respect to "personal information" that the organization collects, uses or discloses in the "course of commercial activities":

- **"Personal information"** is defined as information about an identifiable individual, but does not include business contact information.[53]

- **"Commercial activity"** is defined as any transaction, act or conduct, or any regular course of conduct that is of a commercial character, including the selling, bartering or leasing of donor, membership or other fundraising lists.

The principles behind PIPEDA are similar to the Code of Fair Information Practices discussed in Chapter 1. The act requires organizations to adhere to 10 standards regarding the information that they collect. These 10 standards were previously developed and adopted in 1996 by the Canadian Standards Association as a voluntary industry code called the Model Code for the Protection of Personal Information.[54]

Under PIPEDA, an organization is prohibited from using personal information without the person's consent except in particular situations, such as for law enforcement investigations and emergency situations. Similarly, an organization is prohibited from disclosing personal information without consent, except in particular situations, such as for debt collection, for compliance with a law or court order, or for law enforcement or national security purposes.

Oversight of PIPEDA is conducted on the national level by the Office of the Information and Privacy Commissioner of Canada, located in Ottawa, Ontario.[55] The commissioner has broad powers to enforce the act. For example, the commissioner can audit any organization collecting personal information on Canadian citizens and has the power to investigate, compel the production of evidence, make findings and recommendations and take such cases to the courts for judicial action. Individuals may also hold organizations liable for violations of the act, seeking injunctive relief and/or monetary damages.

PIPEDA also provides for the enactment of provincial privacy legislation, and each province has an active, independent data protection authority. If a provincial law is deemed "substantially similar" to PIPEDA, it generally supersedes PIPEDA with respect to the regulation of intraprovincial and provincial government activities. At present, the provinces of Alberta, British Columbia and Quebec have substantially similar laws that govern the private sector.[56] The "substantially similar" text enables the enactment of locally appropriate laws that are harmonized with and substantially similar to the federal law. The province of Ontario's health law, the Personal Health Information Protection Act, has also been deemed to be substantially similar.

4.2.2 Latin America

The Latin American region includes more than 30 countries. Privacy rights in some instances are provided by constitutional guarantees or amendments to the existing constitutional laws of these countries. Over time, some countries have adopted privacy and data protection laws modeled on the EU Directive, the APEC framework or the OECD Guidelines. Other countries, including Brazil, have not to date issued general data protection laws.

The constitutional process began in Brazil in 1990 with a formal amendment to the Brazilian Constitution in order to permit the right of citizen access to personal information. This continued throughout the 1990s with similar provisions in the constitutions of Colombia, Paraguay, Venezuela, Ecuador and Uruguay. Common themes under these constitutional provisions include:

- A constitutional mandate to ensure privacy

- A traditional privacy clause

- A definition of sensitive personal information

- The right for citizens to rectify information

- An express consent requirement

- A provision for "habeas data"

Privacy and data protection laws in Latin America are generally based on rights of habeas data. These are constitutional guarantees that the citizenry may "have the data" archived about them by governmental and commercial repositories. This translates into individual rights to compel organizations to provide access to data and, generally, includes rights to mandate correction of inaccurate data and to limit distribution (or mandate destruction) of the data.

Habeas data rights cover both consumer and employee personal information. They do not generally include specific restrictions on the international transfer of personal information. Instead, organizations subject to these rules would likely be required to provide access and respect the other habeas data rights with regard to data maintained anywhere.

The habeas data doctrine varies from country to country, but generally is designed to protect the image, privacy, honor, information, self-determination and freedom of information of a person. In many Latin American countries, habeas data rights are being supplemented with statutory rights in traditional data protection legislation such as the laws in force across the European Union and defined earlier in this chapter.

4.2.2.1 Argentina

Argentina's historical approach to privacy and data protection in many ways mirrors the European experience. In 1994, as a reaction to government abuses, including the forced detainment of political foes (the *desaparecidos*, or "disappeared"), Argentina amended its Constitution to include a right of habeas data, making the protection of personal data a fundamental right.

In 2000, Argentina passed the Law for the Protection of Personal Data (LPPD). This law, which came into effect in 2001, is based on the Argentinean Constitution, and conforms to the EU Data Protection Directive. The law applies to all personal information recorded in files, records and databases, either public or private, and contains provisions relating to general data protection principles, the rights of data subjects, the obligations of data controllers and data users, the supervisory authority, sanctions, and rules of procedure in seeking habeas data as a judicial remedy. It applies, to the extent relevant, to data relating to legal entities. The law also prohibits the international transfer of personal information to nations without "adequate protection." Argentina was one of the first countries for which the EU found an adequate level of protection for purposes of data transfer from the EU. Argentina's data protection law is enforced by a government agency, the National Directorate for the Protection of Personal Data.

4.2.2.2 The Bahamas

In April 2003, the Data Protection Act was passed; however, it did not come into effect until April 2, 2007. The act implements privacy principles established by OECD Guidelines that protect privacy and the flow of personal data. It requires that information be obtained by fair and lawful means and used in a manner consistent with the purpose for which it was collected. The act enables individuals to require persons who collect and use personal data to abide by standards of confidentiality in respect of such data and, upon request, to provide individuals with information it keeps about them. The act prohibits the transfer of personal data to jurisdictions with inadequate data protection laws, except with the data subject's consent.

4.2.2.3 Chile

In 1999, Chile enacted Law No. 19.628—Protection of Private Life or Protection of Personal Data. This law applies to the treatment of personal data in records or data banks by public bodies or individuals and mandates that sensitive personal data cannot be stored in a database, even with the consent of the data subject. Data subjects are entitled to request their information from the data bank holder (either public or private), demand the removal of outdated information and the correction of incorrect data, and request information about the source of the data and addressee, purpose of the storage of the data and identification of the entities or persons to whom the data subject's information is regularly transmitted. While the law as enacted did not create a data protection authority, at time of this writing, Bill of Law No. 6120-07 would create a council to oversee data protection. If that law is enacted, the council would be entitled to suggest legal and regulatory modifications and be in charge of a data register of public and private institutions.

4.2.2.4 Colombia

The privacy legal framework in Colombia has three main sets of rules: the Constitution, which expressly recognizes the habeas data right as a fundamental right for both individuals and legal entities; Law 1266 of 2008, which regulates financial personal data (i.e., data collected and administered by any person or entity for purposes of credit risk assessment); and a new Data Protection Law, which was approved by Congress in December 2010, subject to review by the Constitutional Court. In October 2011, the Constitutional Court of Colombia approved almost all of the provisions of this law. The Data Protection Law will, when enacted, prohibit the processing of personal data without the data subject's prior consent and permit cross-border transfers of personal data to countries that lack adequate data protection laws only in specified circumstances, such as when the data subject has given express and unequivocal consent for the transfer, the transfer is necessary for the performance of a contract between the data subject and the data controller or the transfer has the approval of the Superintendence of Industry and Commerce.

The Superintendence of Industry and Trade will have jurisdiction over enforcement and compliance with the law relative to the personal information held by private or public entities that does not constitute personal financial data.

4.2.2.5 Costa Rica

Law No. 8968 on the Protection of the Person Concerning the Processing of Personal Data Act entered into force on September 5, 2011. Once the Agency for the Protection of Individual's Data (the "Prodhab") is created, the government will have a maximum of another six months to issue the regulations, and companies will have a one-year grace period to make sure they are compliant with this new law. The law applies to personal data contained in automated databases of public or private agencies and all manner of subsequent uses of the data. It requires that data controllers provide information to data subjects before they can provide consent and that every database, whether public or private, that is administered for the purposes of distribution, disclosure or business administration be registered with the Prodhab.

4.2.2.6 Mexico

In 2010 Mexico passed the Federal Law on the Protection of Personal Data Held by Private Parties. It establishes an omnibus data protection regime similar to the EU Directive. The law contains provisions relating to the rights of data subjects, obligations of data controllers and users, and international transfer requirements; it differs from the EU approach, however, by incorporating the habeas data concept used in several other Latin American legal regimes. The law applies to all private individuals and entities that process personal data but excludes credit bureaus and persons engaged in the collection and storage of personal data for personal use only, and without disclosing or using it for commercial purposes. The law provides that all data controllers must designate a personal data individual or department who will process requests from data subjects for the exercise of the rights.

On December 21, 2011, Mexico's Ministry of Economy issued Regulations to the Federal Law on the Protection of Personal Data Held by Private Parties, which went into effect the following day. The regulations provide for the development of self-regulatory schemes, establish the territorial application of the law and detail obligations of data controllers relative to the data protection principles.

4.2.2.7 Paraguay

Law No. 1682 (as amended in 2002 and 2009) was promulgated in 2001 and regulates the collection, storage, distribution, publication, modification, destruction and processing of personal data contained in files, records, databases or other technical means of treatment of public or private data intended to provide reports. It is directed mainly at commercial information and provides that data explicitly classified as "sensitive" may not be published or disseminated without prior written consent of the individual concerned; nonsensitive data may be disclosed. There are no additional procedures governing the accumulation, retention and release of customer information.

4.2.2.8 Peru

Effective July 4, 2011, the Peruvian Law of Personal Data Protection applies to personal data contained in private or public data banks within Peru (except those created by natural persons for private or family use, or those created by public entities for fulfillment of their responsibilities); prior and informed consent is not needed to process personal data where the personal data is public information or related to the financial solvency or creditworthiness of the person, if the processing is necessary for execution of a contractual relationship or is essential for healthcare. Transgressions of the law are punishable by fines of up to $128,000. International transfers may be made in the absence of adequate levels of protection where it is conducted as part of international judicial cooperation or cooperation among intelligence agencies, for the execution of a contract with the data owner or for bank transfers or exchanges.

4.2.2.9 Trinidad and Tobago

In June 2011, the Parliament of Trinidad and Tobago enacted the Data Protection Act, 2011. The act includes 12 General Privacy Principles that apply to all persons who handle, store or process personal information belonging to another person and to both public bodies and the private sector.

4.2.2.10 Uruguay

Uruguay was the second country in the region to enact an omnibus data protection law, the Personal Data Protection and Habeas Data Action Act 18.331, in 2008. The scope of the act includes personal data registered in any medium that is susceptible of being processed. All persons and legal entities are subject to general privacy principles of legality, veracity, purpose, prior and informed consent, security of data, confidentiality and responsibility. The act prohibits (subject to some exceptions) the transfer of personal data to countries or international organizations that fail to provide adequate levels of protection. The controlling body is the Data Regulation and Control Unit; the act recognizes the right of every person (individuals or legal entities) to bring legal action and to demand correction, inclusion, or deletion in the event of mistake, falsehood, discrimination or outdating.

In October 2011, the European Union's Article 29 Working Party vetted Uruguay as a jurisdiction with adequate protection; consequently, it might soon be considered as "adequate" by the EU Commission.

4.3 Asia/Pacific Outside of Australia

Chapter 1 discussed the Asia-Pacific Economic Cooperation (APEC) Privacy Framework, which has issued nine information privacy principles that generally mirror the OECD Guidelines, but in some areas are more explicit about exceptions. The APEC Privacy Framework is intended to promote interoperability of privacy regimes across the region. National laws in the region, however, vary considerably in their nature, scope and degree of enforcement.

4.3.1 Hong Kong

The Personal Data (Privacy) Ordinance was brought into force in 1996. The ordinance applies to any data user (an individual, company or public entity) in both the public and private sectors that controls the collection, holding, processing or use of personal data. Six data protection principles are contained within the ordinance: purpose and manner of collection, accuracy and duration of retention, use of personal data, security of personal data, information to be generally available and access to personal data. Data subjects have the rights of access to and correction of their data.

4.3.2 India

Privacy and data protection law in India is in a period of extensive change. Some laws have been put forward but then withdrawn or modified, so the precise path for the law going forward is not entirely clear as of early 2012. One area of particular interest is how privacy and security requirements may apply to the large sector in India that supplies services to other countries, including phone center and other back office functions. India to date has also not promulgated privacy laws with respect to the public sector.

In 2011, India's Department of Information Technology released a set of final regulations concerning parts of the Information Technology (Amendment) Act of 2008 related to data security, personal information privacy, service provider due diligence requirements and cyber café guidelines.[57] The result is a data protection regime that affects all "body corporates" that receive, possess, store, retain or otherwise handle personal information in India. "Body corporate" is defined as "any company and includes a firm, sole proprietorship or other association of individuals engaged in commercial or professional activities."[58]

The 2011 Information Technology (Reasonable Security Practices and Procedures and Sensitive Personal Data or Information) Rules create many new responsibilities for entities, including the requirement of privacy policies and restrictions on the processing of sensitive data and international data transfers. The rules apply to any company or person located in India that processes sensitive personal data. However, certain consent and disclosure requirements do not apply to companies or persons that process sensitive personal data on behalf of any other company located within or outside of India.[59] A few of the key provisions are as follows:

- **Privacy policy.** Any entity that "collects, receives, possesses, stores, deals or handles" personal information must provide a privacy policy to individuals. The policy must clearly detail its information management practices, identify sensitive personal data collected, specify and explain the purpose for which the information is being collected and will be used and implement reasonable security measures to protect the information.

- **Data collection and processing restrictions.** When the information is collected, entities must notify individuals that sensitive information is being collected and provide the purpose of its use, the intended recipients of the data and contact information for the agencies collecting and retaining the data. Personal data may be processed only for its specified purpose.

- **Access and right to correct.** Individuals have the right to access and correct their personal information.

- **Additional restrictions on sensitive data.** The rules define "sensitive personal data" to include physical, physiological and mental health conditions, medical records, sexual orientation, biometric information, passwords and financial information. Prior to collection, entities must obtain written consent from individuals regarding the purpose of use. The individual has the right to withdraw consent, which must be sent in writing to the entity. Consent must also be obtained before sensitive information can be transferred to third parties. Sensitive information may be processed only for its specified purpose.

- **International data transfers.** Entities may transfer personal information only to countries that maintain the same level of data protection, or if in accordance with a legal contract or an individual's consent.

- **Security.** Entities must implement reasonable security measures to effectively protect personal information, commensurate with the information being protected and the nature of the business. The information security program must be well documented. If a security breach occurs, the entity must demonstrate that it implemented appropriate security measures.

4.3.3 Indonesia

Indonesia has not enacted a comprehensive data protection or privacy law. The country did enact Law No. 11 of 2008 regarding electronic transactions and information on April 21, 2008. A provision within the law (Article 26) requires the consent of data subjects prior to the electronic use of their personal data and provides compensation for any person whose rights under the statute are violated.[60]

4.3.4 Japan

Data protection rules vary significantly by sector in Japan, similar in that respect to the U.S. approach. The Law Concerning the Protection of Personal Information was enacted in 2003 and became effective for private sector entities in 2005. The law represents one part of a complex privacy regulatory regime, which differs in important details from the laws in other countries. It is implemented through guidelines promulgated by the various ministries charged with the enforcement of the law within their respective industry sectors.[61]

Japan's law contains several key definitions:

- **"Personal information"** means information that relates to living individuals and which can be used to identify specific individuals by name, date of birth or other description (including data that can easily be compared with other information and thereby be used to identify specific individuals).

- **"Personal information database"** refers to the collection of information, including personal information, defined as (a) information that is structurally constituted so that specific personal information can easily be retrieved by use of a computer and (b) manual or paper-based records that are structurally constituted so that specific personal information can easily be retrieved.

- **"Businesses handling personal information"** refers to an entity that uses personal information databases for business operations. Certain exceptions exist, including "persons designated by government ordinance as being little or no threat to the rights or welfare of individuals from the standpoint of the quantity of personal information handled and the method of use."[62]

- **"Personal data"** refers to personal information that makes up a personal information database.

- **"Held personal data"** generally refers to personal data over which a business handling personal information has the authority to disclose; to make corrections, additions or deletions of content; to cease use; to eliminate; or to cease providing to third parties.

- **"Principal"** with respect to personal information refers to the specific individual identified by personal information (i.e., the data subject). Additionally, the definition of "third parties" is also critical for understanding the data transfer provisions of the Japanese law. All separate legal entities are third parties, even if they are related to (or affiliated with) an organization. The definition of third parties does not, however, apply to "delegates" or true data processors that handle data only pursuant to the instructions of the original organization.

Japan's law sets forth a general approach for privacy protection, called the Basic Policy, which outlines the following duties of businesses handling personal information, including:

- Specification of and limitation on the "purpose of use"
- Appropriate (fair) acquisition of personal information
- Notification of the purpose of use (at collection)
- Securing accuracy of data content
- Security control measures
- Supervision of employees and delegates (data processors)
- Restrictions on providing information to third parties
- Public announcement of items relating to held personal data
- Disclosure (access), correction, cease use, etc.
- Explanation of reasons (for refusal to correct, cease use, etc.)
- Procedures for responding to request for disclosure
- Processing of grievances by businesses handling personal information
- Collection of reports and advice (ministerial notification and guidance)
- Admonishments and orders (enforcement)

Japan's law does not provide any specific regulation of international transfers, and so its approach to this issue, for an economically important country, merits discussion. Japan instead imposes strong consent-based requirements on all transfers of personal information to third parties, regardless of the location of the recipient. Additionally, as noted above, the restrictions on transfer apply to all third parties (other than delegates), including affiliated entities.[63]

In particular, the law stipulates that businesses handling personal information shall not provide personal data to any third party without first acquiring the explicit consent of the principal.[64] The law does provide for certain transfers outside of this rule, including transfers to delegates as needed to achieve the purpose of use, transfers in connection with business succession operations (such as mergers) and transfers in connection with joint use arrangements, if certain conditions are met.

Additionally, while the general rule requires explicit consent for transfers, the law does provide a mechanism for companies to share personal information using an opt-out regime. A company may transfer personal data if the company has provided notice to the principal stating (1) that the transfer of personal data to third parties is included in the purpose of use; (2) the categories of personal data that will be provided; (3) the means and methods of transferring the personal data; and (4) that the principal can, upon request, have the business cease transfer of the personal data to the third parties.

It is important to note that the ministerial regulations may provide additional limitations on the data transfers. The various guidelines also address issues of corporate accountability for transfers. The transfer rules clearly imply that businesses are accountable for actions of delegates regardless of where those entities reside. Similarly, with respect to human resources data, Guidelines from the Ministry of Economy, Trade and Industry and the Ministry of Health, Labor and Welfare provide that companies remain accountable for the processing of personal information by third parties even if the principal has explicitly consented to the transfer.

4.3.5 Kyrgyz Republic

The Law of the Kyrgyz Republic on Personal Data became effective in 2008 and applies to both the private and public sectors. Basic principles contained within the law address the legitimate processing of data; the collection of data for specific, declared and lawful purposes (and not secondary purposes); data accuracy; and security.

4.3.6 Macau

The Personal Data Protection Act (Act 8/2005) applies to the public and private sectors and regulates the processing of sensitive data; contains provisions regarding prior checking, data quality, security and the transfer of data outside Macau; contains notice and consent requirements; and provides data subjects with the rights of access, objection and legal recourse.

4.3.7 Malaysia

The Personal Data Protection Act 2010 has not come into effect as of early 2012. The act will cover the public and private sectors and contain seven data protection principles, including the general principle establishing legal requirements for processing personal data (e.g., with consent or to comply with legal requirements), notice (internal privacy notices for employees and external notices for consumers), choice (individuals have the right to withdraw their consent to processing), data security, and cross-border transfers (modeled on the EU's Data Protection Directive).[65]

4.3.8 Mongolia

The Law on Personal Secrecy (Privacy Law) of Mongolia allows only officials of authorized state organizations access to personal data of citizens that is kept in accordance with procedures and on grounds determined by law.[66]

4.3.9 New Zealand

New Zealand has a co-regulatory approach to privacy, broadly similar to Australia's. The Privacy Act 1993 applies to both the public and private sectors and contains 12 privacy principles covering collection of personal information, storage and security, requests for access and correction, accuracy, retention, use and disclosure and using unique identifiers. There are also four principles covering public registers. In addition, the act includes privacy Codes of Practice that apply to specific industries—for example, health, telecommunications and credit reporting.

4.3.10 Singapore

Singapore has not enacted a comprehensive privacy or data protection law. However, in 2011 the government announced that it was taking steps to introduce a data protection law in 2012.[67] The government is also making plans to establish a regulatory regime to oversee implementation and enforcement of the legislation.

4.3.11 South Korea

The Personal Information Protection Act came into effect on September 30, 2011, and applies to the collection and handling of personal information in both the public and private sectors. The act contains provisions for a data handler to obtain a data subject's consent for the collection, use or disclosure of his or her personal information.

4.3.12 Taiwan

Previously, Taiwan's Computer-Processed Personal Data Protection Act (CPPDPA) applied only to government agencies, hospitals, schools and private companies in certain industries. However, an amendment passed in May 2010 makes CPPDPA applicable to all private companies.[68] Among other requirements and obligations, CPPDPA requires written consent from employees whose personal data is collected, processed, used or transmitted, with few exceptions. Before providing written consent, employees must be informed of specific information regarding the entities that will have access to the information. The law also includes enhanced protection for "sensitive" data and imposes limits on international transfers of information. Taiwan also introduced a revised draft Data Protection Act in 2011, making it the first privacy-oriented data breach notification law in the APEC region.[69]

4.3.13 Thailand

The Official Information Act, B.E. 2540 (1997), effective in 1997, applies to the public sector. The principle of the act is the guarantee of the people's rights to have full access to government information and provides a right to appeal to the Official Information Commission should the state agency deny disclosure of some excepted data.

4.4 Middle East

4.4.1 Dubai

The Data Protection Law of 2007, which strengthened a previous 2004 law, creates rules regarding the collection, handling, disclosure and use of personal data and the rights of individuals to whom the personal data belongs. The law protects all personal and sensitive information and is consistent with EU directives and the OECD Guidelines.

4.4.2 Israel

Israel has a number of laws that regulate privacy, two of which are particularly relevant to information privacy. First, the Basic Law on Human Dignity and Freedom establishes a broad right to privacy. Israel does not have a written constitution, although its body of "basic laws" has constitutional status.[70] In reference to privacy, Section 7 of Israel's Basic Law on Human Dignity and Liberty (1992) states:

(a) *All persons have the right to privacy and to intimacy;*

(b) *There shall be no entry into the private premises of a person who has not consented thereto;*

(c) *No search shall be conducted on the private premises or body of a person, nor in the body or belongings of a person;*

(d) *There shall be no violation of the secrecy of the spoken utterances, writings or records of a person.*[71]

Second, the Protection of Privacy Law of 1981 acts as a data protection framework and consists of two main elements. Chapter 1 or "the Privacy Law" sets out general privacy protection laws. Chapter 2, "Protection of Privacy in Databases," provides extensive protection for individual data collected on a database, and more closely resembles information data protection laws that exist in Europe and elsewhere in the world. Chapter 1 specifies 11 categories of privacy breaches and enumerates the corresponding civil and criminal penalties.[72] Chapter 2 requires information databases to be registered with the Israeli government if the database meets one of the following criteria:

(1) *the database includes information about more than 10,000 persons;*

(2) *the database includes sensitive information;*

(3) *the database includes information about persons and the information was not provided to the database by them, on their behalf, or with their consent;*

(4) *the database belongs to a public body; or*

(5) *the database is used for direct mail.*[73]

Section 13 of Chapter 2 provides individuals the right to inspect their personal information that is stored in a database. Section 14 permits an individual to amend or request that the data be deleted if the data is not correct, complete, clear or up to date. The law also provides judicial process if the owner of the database denies this request.

The Protection of Privacy Regulations (the Transfer of Information to a Database Outside the State Borders) of 2001 prohibits the transfer of information from a database in Israel to a database in a foreign country unless that country provides a level of protection equivalent to that provided under Israeli law.

In January 2011 the European Commission issued a decision (2011/61/EU) elevating Israel to the list of countries deemed to have an adequate level of protection.

4.5 Africa

A number of African countries in recent years have passed data protection laws, and others are considering proposed laws. As in other parts of the world with new privacy regimes, staffing for data protection authorities may not be extensive, and it may take time before enforcement is widespread.

4.5.1 Angola

Law 22/11 on Personal Data Protection was passed on June 17, 2011. The omnibus privacy law applies to the processing of personal data by controllers based or operating in Angola (public or private sector) or subject to, or using equipment governed by, Angola's laws. The law sets forth data processing principles, including transparency, lawfulness, proportionality, purpose, accuracy and length of retention period. Processing personal data is permitted only with the express consent of the data subject and notification to the Data Protection Agency. International data transfers to countries that do not ensure an adequate level of protection require approval.[74]

4.5.2 Benin

The data protection law in effect is the Law on the Protection of Personal Data.[75]

4.5.3 Burkina Faso

The Data Protection Act was adopted in April 2004 and covers the public and private sectors.[76]

4.5.4 Cape Verde

The data protection law in effect is Law No. 133/V/2201 of 22 January 2001.[77]

4.5.5 Mauritius

The Data Protection Act of 2004, applicable to the public and private sectors, contains eight data protection principles (including fair and lawful processing, proportionate collection, data accuracy and retention, security measures and cross-border transfers) and includes provisions regarding the registration of data controllers and processors and rights of access for data subjects.[78]

4.5.6 Morocco

Law No. 09-08 on the Protection of Individuals with regard to the treatment of personal data became effective in 2009 and applies to the public and private sectors. The law introduced a set of legal provisions aimed at protecting the identity, rights and individual and collective freedoms as well as privacy against all attacks that may affect individuals through the use of computers. The law defines the right of access to databases containing personal data, to object to certain treatments and to request correction of erroneous data and delete outdated information.[79]

4.5.7 Senegal

Law No. 2008-12 on the Protection of Personal Data was entered into force in 2008 and applies to the public and private sectors. The law contains general provisions on the protection of personal data as well as obligations for data controllers and addresses the rights of the individual whose data is being processed.[80]

4.5.8 Tunisia

The Data Protection Act (No. 2004-63), effective July 27, 2004, which appears to apply only to the private sector, establishes that citizens have a right to privacy and protection of their personal data.[81] The act is based on the EU Data Protection Directive 95/46/EC.

4.5.9 Zimbabwe

The Access to Information and Protection of Privacy Act applies to the public sector and was enacted on March 15, 2002.[82]

5. Role of the Data Protection and Privacy Authorities

The actual effectiveness of these many laws depends in part on the officials and agencies responsible for supervision and enforcement.[83] In countries with comprehensive and co-regulatory approaches, names for these officials include data protection authority (DPA, a commonly used term throughout Europe), privacy commissioner (as in Canada, Hong Kong and New Zealand) and information commissioner (in the United Kingdom and Australia). In countries with a sectoral approach, including the United States and Japan, different agencies or officials have responsibility for different sectors, such as for healthcare privacy, financial privacy and general online privacy.

Responsibilities of these officials include validating compliance with the law, investigating alleged breaches of the law's provisions, educating the public on data protection matters and acting as an international liaison for data protection issues. Data protection officials are granted varying degrees of enforcement power from country to country; some of their powers are the ability to audit entities for compliance, impose a ban on processing activities, suspend flows of personal information to third countries, warn or admonish noncompliant entities and levy fines.

In practice, countries choose to allocate varying levels of resources to the enforcement of data protection laws, with the result that officials in some countries are not funded adequately to meet the stated goals of the laws. Nonetheless, privacy and data protection professionals should inform themselves of the variety of national laws that apply to the processing of personal data by their organization. For countries with existing privacy and data protection rules, there has been a clear trend over time toward greater enforcement and higher fines for violations. The regulation proposed for the European Union in January 2012 highlighted this trend, providing that fines could go up to two percent of a company's global turnover (revenue), with the potential of fines totaling many millions or even billions of dollars/euros going forward.[84] In an era where personal information routinely crosses borders, professionals increasingly must become alert to international rules and norms for the processing of personal information.

6. Summary

This chapter has provided an introduction to the variety of privacy and data protection laws around the world. Significant privacy and data protection laws existed in a number of countries before promulgation of the EU Data Protection Directive in 1995, but such laws were concentrated in Europe, North America and a few other nations. Since that time, privacy and data protection laws have spread to all regions of the world, with a majority of the laws, now in over 80 countries, put into place in the past decade.

Endnotes

1 "Graham Greenleaf's Global Table of Data Privacy Laws," accessed Nov. 8, 2011, www2.austlii.edu.au/~graham/DP_Table/DP_TABLE.html.

2 David Banisar and Simon Davies, "Global Trends in Privacy Protection: An International Survey of Privacy, Data Protection, and Surveillance Laws and Developments," *John Marshall Journal of Computer and Information Law* 18 (Fall 1999).

3 *Id.* at 14.

4 *Id.* at 11.

5 *Id.* at 14.

6 Section 13 of Ireland's Data Protection Acts, 1998 and 2003, set out the process by which trade associations and other bodies can seek approval of codes of practice from the Data Protection Commissioner, which may then be laid before Parliament. If each house of Parliament passes a resolution approving a code of practice, the code then has the force of law.

7 Banisar and Davies, "Global Trends," 13–14.

8 www.gsma.com/documents/mobile-privacy-principles/20005/.

9 www.privacyalliance.org/.

10 Major R. Ken Pippin, "Consumer Privacy on the Internet: It's 'Surfer Beware,'" *Air Force L. Rev.* 47 (1999): 125, 131.

11 "Commentary to the Mission Statement and Guidelines," Online Privacy Alliance, Nov. 19, 1998, www.privacyalliance.org/news/12031998-4.shtml.

12 *Id.* at 132.

13 *Id.* See also Federal Trade Commission, "Self-Regulation and Online Privacy: A Report to Congress," July 1, 1999, 6, www.ftc.gov/os/1999/07/privacy99.pdf.

14 http://eur-lex.europa.eu/LexUriServ/LexUriServ.do?uri=CELEX:31995L0046:en:HTML.

15 www.ico.gov.uk/upload/documents/library/data_protection/detailed_specialist_guides/160408_v1.0_determining_what_is_personal_data_-_quick_reference_guide.pdf.

16 For extensive discussion of the rules for transfers of personal data to third countries, see Peter P. Swire and Robert E. Litan, *None of Your Business: World Data Flows, Electronic Commerce, and the European Privacy Directive*, (Washington, DC: Brookings Institution Press, 1998).

17 Article 25.1 of the Directive 95/46/EC provides that "the transfer to a third country of personal data which are undergoing processing or are intended for processing after transfer may take place only if . . . the third country in question ensures an adequate level of data protection."

18 http://ec.europa.eu/justice/policies/privacy/thridcountries/index_en.htm. In addition to the countries listed, adequacy determinations have been made for transfers to the United States within the Safe Harbor framework, pursuant to certain model contracts and within the Air Passenger Name Record data agreement.

19 http://ec.europa.eu/justice/policies/privacy/docs/wpdocs/2008/wp153_en.pdf.

20 97/66/EC of the European Parliament and of the Council of 15 December 1997 concerning the processing of personal data and the protection of privacy in the telecommunications sector.

21 Traditional (manual) telemarketing remained subject to the general Data Protection Directive's notice and opt-out provisions.

22 2002/58/EC, Directive of the European Parliament of the Council of 12 July 2002 concerning the processing of personal data and the protection of privacy in the electronic communications sector, http://eur-lex.europa.eu/LexUriServ/LexUriServ.do?uri=OJ:L:2002:201:0037:0037:EN:PDF.

23 http://ec.europa.eu/justice/data-protection/article-29/index_en.htm.

24 This enforcement scheme has resulted in certain U.S. industries being ineligible for Safe Harbor certification. For example, because the FTC and DOT do not have jurisdiction to regulate banks and other financial institutions, these types of entities are not eligible for the Safe Harbor. (These entities are exclusively regulated by other federal and state regulators, who have not agreed to enforce Safe Harbor promises.

25 http://export.gov/safeharbor/.

26 EU model contracts for the transfer of personal data to third countries, http://ec.europa.eu/justice/policies/privacy/modelcontracts/index_en.htm.

27 http://export.gov/safeharbor/swiss/index.asp.

28 Courts have found privacy protections in the 1st, 4th, 5th, and 14th Amendments. See generally http://netsecurity.about.com/od/newsandeditorial1/a/aaprivacyrights.htm.

29 Samuel Warren and Louis Brandeis, "The Right to Privacy," *Harv. L. Rev.* 4 (1890): 193, 215.

30 William Prosser, "Privacy," *Cal. L. Rev.* 48 (1960): 383.

31 Restatement (Second) of Torts at §§ 652A-652I (1977).

32 *Griswold v. Connecticut,* 381 US 479 (1965).

33 *Roe v. Wade,* 410 US 113 (1973).

34 *Lawrence and Garner v. Texas*, 539 US 558 (2003).

35 www.gpo.gov/fdsys/pkg/PLAW-106publ102/pdf/PLAW-106publ102.pdf.

36 Federal Trade Commission, Fair Credit Reporting Act, www.ftc.gov/os/statutes/fcra.htm.

37 U.S. Department of Health, Education and Welfare, "Records, Computers, and the Rights of Citizens: Report of the Secretary's Advisory Committee on Automated Personal Data Systems," July 1973, viii.

38 The White House, "Consumer Data Privacy in a Networked World: A Framework for Protecting Privacy and Promoting Innovation in the Global Digital Economy," February 2012, www.whitehouse.gov/sites/default/files/privacy-final.pdf.

39 Center for Democracy and Technology, "Privacy Basics: Generic Principles of Fair Information Practices." For a slightly different drafting of the principles see Federal Trade Commission, "Fair Information Principles," www.ftc.gov/reports/privacy3/fairinfo.htm.

40 Gramm-Leach-Bliley Act, 15 USC, Subchapter I, Sec. 6801-6809 (1999). Also see FTC, "In Brief: The Financial Privacy Requirements of the Gramm-Leach-Bliley Act," http://business.ftc.gov/sites/default/files/pdf/bus53-brief-financial-privacy-requirements-gramm-leach-bliley-act.pdf.

41 Children's Online Privacy Protection Act of 2000, 15 USC 6501.

42 For an excellent summary of FOIA, see www.epic.org/open_gov/rights.html.

43 *Id.*

44 www.gpo.gov/fdsys/pkg/PLAW-104publ231/pdf/PLAW-104publ231.pdf.

45 See the 11 Information Privacy Principles at www.privacy.gov.au/publications/ipps.html.

46 www.privacy.gov.au/act/privacyact/index.html.

47 See the 10 National Privacy Principles at www.privacy.gov.au/publications/npps01.html.

48 People's Republic of China Constitution (Constitution Act, 1993), Chapter II (Fundamental Rights and Duties of Citizens), Article 40, translation available at www.usconstitution.net/china.html#Article40.

49 *Id.* at Article 38, www.usconstitution.net/china.html#Article38.

50 Christopher Wolf, "China Publishes Draft Privacy Guidelines," *Chronicle of Data Protection,* April 14, 2011, www.hldataprotection.com/2011/04/articles/international-eu-privacy/china-publishes-draft-privacy-guidelines/.

51 Privacy Legislation in Canada, www.priv.gc.ca/fs-fi/02_05_d_15_e.cfm.

52 http://laws-lois.justice.gc.ca/eng/acts/P-8.6/index.html.

53 The types of data elements commonly found on a business card are excluded from coverage of the act.

54 Canadian Standards Association, "Model Code for the Protection of Personal Information," www.csa.ca/cm/ca/en/privacy-code/publications/view-privacy-code.

55 Office of the Privacy Commissioner of Canada, www.priv.gc.ca/.

56 www.priv.gc.ca/legislation/ss_index_e.cfm.

57 2011 Information Technology (Reasonable Security Practices and Procedures and Sensitive Personal Data or Information) Rules, www.mit.gov.in/sites/upload_files/dit/files/RNUS_CyberLaw_15411.pdf.

58 *Id.*

59 Press Note, Clarification on Information Technology (Reasonable Security Practices and Procedures and Sensitive Personal Data or Information) Rules, 2011 Under Section 43A of the Information Technology Act, 2000, http://pib.nic.in/newsite/erelease.aspx?relid=74990.

60 www.asialaw.com/Article/2004303/Channel/17441/The-law-on-electronic-transactions-and-information-a-general-outline.html.

61 Implementing guidelines are issued by the Ministry of Economy, Trade and Industry, the Ministry of Health, Labor and Welfare, the Financial Services Agency, the Ministry of Finance, the Ministry of Internal Affairs and Communications, the Ministry of Land, Infrastructure and Transport, and the Ministry of Justice.

62 For example, databases with fewer than 5,000 records are not covered by the law.

63 Transfers to mere data processors or delegates are not subject to these requirements, as the supervision of the delegates remains with the original organization.

64 A few narrow exceptions exist, such as for transfers made pursuant to a law or ordinance, or as necessary for the protection of human life, safety or property, and when it is difficult to obtain the consent of the principal.

65 "Privacy Background and Hot Topics for Malaysia," an interview with Boris Segalis, Partner, InfoLaw Group LLP, February 22, 2011. Available upon request from Nymity Inc., www.nymity.com.

66 https://www.privacyinternational.org/article/phr2006-mongolia.

67 Shamma Iqbal, "Singapore to Introduce Data Protection Law," Inside Privacy, May 13, 2011, www.insideprivacy.com/international/singapore-to-introduce-data-protection-law/.

68 H. Henry Chang and Chris H. C. Tsai, "Taiwan's New Personal Data Protection Law," Baker & McKenzie, October 2010, www.bakermckenzie.com/RRTaiwanPersonalDataProtectionLawOct10/.

69 Shamma Iqbal, "Taiwan Introduces Enforceable Data Breach Notification Requirements," Inside Privacy, March 9, 2011, www.insideprivacy.com/international/tawain-introduces-enforceable-data-breach-notification-requirements/.

70 "The State: The Law of the Land," Israel Ministry of Foreign Affairs, November 28, 2010, www.mfa.gov.il/MFA/Facts%20About%20Israel/State/THE%20STATE-%20The%20Law%20of%20the%20Land.

71 "Basic Law: Human Dignity and Liberty" (5752 - 1992), passed by the Knesset on the 21st Adar, 5754, March 17, 1992, www.mfa.gov.il/MFA/MFAArchive/1990_1999/1992/3/Basic%20Law-%20Human%20Dignity%20and%20Liberty-.

72 The Protection of Privacy Law 5741-198, 1011 Laws of the State of Israel 128, www.mofo.com/docs/mofoprivacy/Privacy%20Law.doc.

73 Id.

74 www.huntonprivacyblog.com/2011/09/articles/angola-passes-personal-data-protection-law/#more-1888.

75 http://allafrica.com/stories/201111110235.html.

76 www.privacyconference2009.org/dpas_space/space_reserved/documentos_adoptados/common/report_credentials_committee_en.pdf.

77 http://lawbrain.com/wiki/Africa_Privacy_Law#Cape_Verde.

78 www.gov.mu/portal/goc/dpo/files/DPA2004v6.doc.

79 www.invest.gov.ma/?lang=en&Id=17.

80 www.wipo.int/wipolex/en/text.jsp?file_id=181186.

81 https://www.privacyinternational.org/article/tunisia-adopts-data-protection-act.

82 www.sokwanele.com/pdfs/AIPPA.pdf.

83 Banisar and Davies, "Global Trends," 14.

84 See Article 79 of the Proposal for a Regulation of the European Parliament and of the Council on the Protection of Individuals with Regard to Processing of Personal Data and on the Free Movement of Such Data, http://ec.europa.eu/justice/data-protection/document/review2012/com_2012_11_en.pdf.

CHAPTER THREE

Sectors of Privacy
and Data Protection Law

Not all types of personal information are created equal. Going back generations, there have been special confidentiality rules for certain types of sensitive data, including medical and financial data. As practitioners learn about modern privacy and data protection rules, they should be aware that additional and specialized rules may apply in these sensitive areas. This chapter discusses important sectors of privacy and data protection, notably medical confidentiality; financial privacy; telecommunication laws; online activity regulations; and rules that apply to governments, human resource management, smart grid and smart home issues, and direct marketing.

1. Healthcare Sector

Special privacy protections for healthcare date back thousands of years. The modern Hippocratic oath states, "I will respect the privacy of my patients, for their problems are not disclosed to me that the world may know."[1] The concept of doctor-patient confidentiality exists in many countries as a matter of both tradition and law. Many countries also have specific healthcare privacy laws that they have enacted over time. The Health Insurance Portability and Accountability Act (HIPAA) is a prominent example of the sector-specific approach the United States takes towards privacy. Under the EU Data Protection Directive, healthcare is also singled out as "sensitive" data. Article 8 of the Directive specifically provides that member states can impose stricter rules for health-related information. Provinces in Canada and other countries also have specific healthcare laws providing for stringent privacy protection. Accordingly, privacy practitioners who encounter healthcare information during the course of their work should be alert to the possibility that special rules may apply.

There are several reasons why strict privacy and data protection laws are necessary for healthcare privacy information. First, at the most basic level, medical information is related to the inner workings of one's body or mind. One's individual sense of self may be violated if others have unfettered access to this information. Second, most doctors believe that patients will be more open about their medical conditions if patients have assurance that embarrassing medical facts will not be revealed. Third, medical privacy protections can protect employees from the risk of unequal treatment by employers. For instance, a person who has had an abortion, contracted a sexually transmitted disease or had psychiatric treatment could potentially be fired if a prejudiced employer gained access to this information. In countries where the employer pays for health insurance, companies may have financial incentives to avoid employing workers who suffer from expensive medical conditions or who may be at higher risk of expensive conditions based on their genetic background.

Despite the existence of strict laws protecting medical information, modern medical practice often uses patient medical information quite intensively. For example, information about medical procedures is frequently used to assure accurate payment for those services. Doctors in one location may wish to access records about a patient's medical treatment in other cities in order to treat the patient appropriately. Researchers also use medical information, sometimes de-identified, in trying to find new patterns as they seek to develop cures for illnesses and promote public health.

2. Financial Sector

Banking and other financial records have long been treated with high levels of confidentiality. Medieval and early modern banks often kept the identity of their borrowers secret and would not reveal intimate financial details of their customers. One reason for this confidentiality was to encourage borrowers to report honestly to the lender about their other debts and ability to pay. Another priority in the financial sector is to assure security—thieves and fraudsters can target individuals or transactions if they have access to these details.

Today, many countries use sector-specific rules both to protect the privacy of financial information and to ensure that information is appropriately shared with the government and other related players. In the United States, the Gramm-Leach-Bliley Act of 1999 established a complicated set of privacy and security requirements for all financial institutions.[2] In Japan, the Act on the Protection of Personal Information and accompanying guidelines regulate the use of customers' personal information in the financial services sector.[3] Also, many countries have historically used "bank secrecy" laws, which prohibit banks from turning over details about their customers, especially to authorities in other countries who are seeking to enforce tax or other laws. Switzerland is famous for its bank secrecy laws; however, those rules have relaxed over time. Today, various "offshore" jurisdictions carry on extensive financial activities and continue to use bank secrecy laws.

Recently, enforcement against money laundering has resulted in greater government access to financial records, both within each nation and internationally. The global focus on fighting terrorism has accelerated the spread of money-laundering laws with the goal of preventing or detecting flows of funds to international terrorists. Major country economies have also put pressure on the offshore countries to reveal financial records, as a way to both fight terrorism and enforce their tax laws.

Privacy and security experts in the financial system, therefore, must remain aware of the requirements for both confidentiality and disclosure. Specialized financial rules can apply either to financial institutions or to financial transactions, and differ depending on the type of institution or transaction. For example, security measures for banks are often subject to different rules and the scrutiny of different oversight agencies than other institutions because of the higher risk of theft and the need for oversight by bank regulators. Money-laundering laws apply to many organizations, from casinos to car dealers, to encourage government reporting on suspicious financial activities. In addition, rules vary from country to country for reporting on an individual's credit history. Privacy professionals should thus be alert for the possibility of special local rules for information about credit histories.

3. Telecommunications Sector

Telecommunication privacy rules historically applied to wiretaps and other access to telephone activities. Increasingly, telecommunication privacy rules apply to other forms of communication such as e-mail, chat or web surfing. It is easiest to understand the range of modern telecommunications rules by distinguishing three categories. First, wiretaps and similar technologies gain access to the **content** of the communication, such as what people say on the telephone or write in a chat or e-mail. Second is access on an ongoing basis to **to/from information**, identifying each phone number or e-mail address contacted by an individual. Third, **stored telecommunication records** can reveal both content (what an e-mail said last month) and contact information (who sent or received an e-mail or a call to the person last month).

Telecommunication information is highly prized by law enforcement and national security agencies. The to-from information can aid police in identifying possible accomplices or coconspirators. The content of the information, such as that retrieved from a telephone wiretap, can reveal the precise plans and activities of a criminal suspect. Because these records have the potential to be very useful for law enforcement agencies, but are also extremely personal, many countries have passed specific wiretap and related laws to protect the privacy of these communications. These laws typically set standards and establish procedures for government access to the communications. These same laws usually make it a crime for private citizens to wiretap or gain unauthorized access to this information. Additionally, electronic communication and other usage records, such as lists of e-mails sent or phone calls made, are typically subject to specific laws that limit access by nongovernmental actors. To understand the privacy concerns about telecommunications, imagine that your employer or family members could listen to every phone call you made. This form of invasive surveillance could easily chill your willingness to speak openly with the person on the other end of the line.

With the rapid adoption and widespread use of mobile devices in recent years, a fourth category of privacy-sensitive information is becoming increasingly important—**location information**. For the first time in history, people in their everyday lives are carrying a device that reports constantly on their whereabouts. Because widespread use of mobile phones and smartphones is so recent, current debates revolve around who should have access to location information and on what terms.

The growing diversity of telecommunications is accompanied by an increasing range of sector-specific laws and best practice regimes for telephones, e-mails and other forms of communication. The usefulness of location information to the police, marketers and other actors will also continue to foster complex rules about how to provide appropriate access to information while ensuring privacy and security.

4. Online Privacy

The development of the Internet in the 1990s triggered an ongoing international debate about Internet privacy that continues today. On the one hand, special rules for the Internet violate the principle of technology neutrality, which is the concept that citizens' rights should not vary depending on a specific technology. On the other hand, the Internet has created new and considerable challenges to privacy protection. First, many Internet privacy problems seem novel, without easy comparisons to past practice. Today a doctor is still a doctor, and a bank is still a bank, but it is hard to know which historical privacy and data protection rules best apply to Internet activity. Second, the Internet enables far more detailed collection of information than has historically been the case. In the offline world, a newspaper would at most possess knowledge of its customers' names, addresses and subscriptions. On the Internet, by contrast, the newspaper might know exactly which articles were read by which subscribers, providing far more detailed clues as to its users' preferences. This enormous increase in detail is a great aid to companies that wish to personalize their offerings and provide customers with tailored services and product options. This increased detail, however, also raises privacy concerns, especially because many web users do not possess the technological sophistication to understand exactly how their data is being accessed and used.

The third and perhaps most important way in which the Internet differs is its inherently global nature. Historically, individuals made purchases in person, in their hometown or by mail order. With the Internet, however, a single website can sell goods to customers all around the world. The global nature of the Internet greatly increases the likelihood that the privacy and data protection laws of more than one nation may apply to online transactions. As discussed further in Chapter 5, these issues are important to the ongoing discussion and debate about what online privacy rules should exist.

5. Public Sector

Many nations have different requirements and handling procedures for information held by the government than for information held by corporations and other private actors. For example, the EU Data Protection Directive applies to personal information held by both the government and the private sector. Nonetheless, there are different and generally less strict legal rules for "first pillar" government organizations, where the police and other government agencies hold personal information, than for data held by private actors.[4] In the United States, the Privacy Act of 1974 requires federal agencies to apply fair information privacy practices. Canada has three levels of privacy law: federal, province or territory, and municipality.

There are strong reasons supporting both sides of the debate about whether the government should receive more or less access to private information. Reasons supporting broad government access and use include national security and law enforcement, to protect the basic foundations of society. Governments across the world also administer a wide range of social welfare activities such as healthcare, pensions and education. To run those government programs efficiently, managers often need access to a wide array of personal information.

However, there are also important reasons for concern regarding government access and use of personal information. These problems are easiest to see in totalitarian regimes, where state control is nearly absolute and the individual has no right to privacy. One well-known example is that of the Nazis in Germany, who compiled detailed records about assets held by Jewish citizens. The Nazis later used those records to identify and locate Jews in their mass extermination efforts. Even open and democratic societies have a history of using strong legal protections to limit government invasion of privacy. The Fourth Amendment to the U.S. Constitution generally requires proof of probable cause for a crime before a judge will issue a search warrant or wiretap order. Similarly, Article 8 of the EU Convention on Human Rights provides strong privacy rights against illegal searches and other government intrusions. These limits on government surveillance are often justified as a way to prevent governments from becoming too strong, thereby preventing a potential slide toward abuse of power.

As with the other categories of data information in this chapter, privacy and security practitioners should take special notice when a local or national government has access to personal information. The applicable rules and best practices will often differ from those for similar uses of data by the private sector.

Countries also vary dramatically in their definitions of "public record." In Sweden, a person's salary is considered a public record—thus, you can easily access your neighbor's annual income. In the United States, the owner of real estate is a public record, while that is considered private information in many other countries. In general, it is lawful to access and use information that is available publicly in the home country, such as the American landowner or the Swedish employee. But privacy practitioners should be aware that these rules about "public records" vary from country to country.

6. Human Resources

There is a very long tradition of privacy in human resources (HR) data management. Even before the establishment of data protection laws, HR professionals often kept personnel files locked and separate from other organization records. This is because HR professionals routinely handle personal, sometimes sensitive, information, including nationally issued identification numbers, home address and phone numbers, financial information, criminal record checks and medical information. HR professionals often have access to this information even for the most senior management in the firm. Thus, employers and HR professionals have strong incentive to provide robust privacy protection against misuse and unauthorized disclosure.

Confidentiality issues with employee information begin at the application stage, continue during employment and persist even after termination. When job seekers apply to an available position, they may not wish their current employers or coworkers to know they are seeking a new position. Accordingly, HR professionals must handle application information with discretion. If the position is not outside, but within the applicant's current place of employment, HR professionals must ensure the confidentiality of salary and other terms of employment, and limit access to assessment of the candidate. Once a person is hired, HR professionals have access to sensitive information, such as financial information and medical information about the employee or family members, including requests for sick leave. Many organizations also conduct annual reviews of employees, and to ensure candor of those involved, privacy measures must be in place. Finally, when an employee leaves an organization, HR professionals must transfer and retain information using the same care as when the employee worked for the organization.

In short, there are numerous reasons to use discretion and confidentiality in the handling of employee files. The widespread adoption of data protection laws has affected the way HR information is treated. HR information is now considered personal data under the EU Directive and the laws of many other countries. This means that employee information must receive the full set of safeguards that apply to other personal information. By contrast, in the United States and many other countries, there is no omnibus privacy protection for such information. Instead, professional organizations such as the International Association for Human Resource Information Management provide a general code of conduct that all members are bound to.[5] HR professionals in the United States must consider the specific privacy obligations under certain privacy sector laws, such as HIPAA and the Fair Credit Reporting Act, both of which require sensitive information to be handled in a way that preserves privacy. States also have a range of laws that protect employee privacy. In addition to outside regulation, most organizations implement internal privacy procedures that establish administrative, technical and physical security of data.

Organizations with employees stationed in more than one country should also be sensitive to the different jurisdictional rules that apply to employee information. For instance, Germany, Austria and other countries with active works councils and trade unions hold certain rights with respect to processing of personal information, including the right to be notified or consulted before an employer introduces measures that may impact the privacy of employees. Further, collective bargaining agreements may address activities that impact the privacy of employees, such as criminal record checks or drug and alcohol testing. Special rules and protections may also apply for government employees, including civil service regimes that are designed to reduce political interference with government employees.

As in other areas of privacy, individuals in countries that follow the EU approach often have a broader range of legal safeguards than individuals in the United States. For example, workplace computer systems in the U.S. are owned and operated by the employer. Individuals, therefore, do not generally have legal rights to use workplace computers free from the company's supervision. In the EU, by contrast, several countries have ruled that employee e-mail is not subject to unfettered employer access. This is just one example of how the human rights approach in the EU operates in practice and differs from the policies in the United States.

Changes in technology and the work environment raise new privacy issues. The increase in outsourcing of HR functions means that significant amounts of data are being transferred to third parties and other countries. As a result, the risk of potential data security breaches is increased. However, formal vendor security protocols, as well as strict contractual provisions, can help mitigate this risk. The use of strong encryption in data transfer and storage, as well as enhanced loss notification, is now common in vendor negotiation and contracting. Continued technological changes lead to the need for updating and reevaluation of workplace privacy guidelines. The privacy rights of employees in the workplace, in the end, are balanced against legitimate interests of the organization and customers.

7. Smart Grid and Smart Home

The "smart grid" is a recent example of technological innovation that may create privacy issues. The term *smart grid* refers to a new energy system that manages electricity consumption through remote computerization and automation. The traditional electric transmission system required physically sending workers into the field to read customer meters and find where problems existed in the grid. This traditional system raised few privacy problems, because customer information was gathered only at specific time intervals, such as once a month. With the advent of computerized smart grid services, however, electricity service providers, users, or third-party service providers can now continuously monitor and control the use of electricity to each home or business from a remote location. The new system directly benefits consumers, by providing them with granular control and choice over the extent of their energy consumption. The system itself also operates more smoothly, because managers can detect problems and reroute transmission in the event of natural disasters or other interruptions, improve efficiency and quality of electricity delivery, and link energy sources.

Many nations are investing heavily in smart grid technology and adopting regulations to address accompanying privacy concerns. For example, in 2011 Canada released a report entitled "Operationalizing Privacy by Design: The Ontario Smart Grid Case Study," which provides guidance for utilities to build privacy into smart grid technology by way of "Privacy by Design."[6] In the U.S., states are beginning to pass smart grid privacy laws that govern the use and disclosure of data and personal information by utility companies and third parties. Notably, in 2010 California passed a first-in-the-nation consumer protection law regulating use of consumer energy information.[7] In 2011, the EU adopted "Communication Smart Grids: from Innovation to Deployment," policy directions focused on developing technical standards and ensuring data protection for consumers.[8] Also in 2011, the EU issued an Article 29 Working Party Opinion that clarifies the legal framework applying to smart meters.[9]

This innovative technology, however, also raises new privacy issues regarding consumer personal information. Smart readers measure energy use continuously, rather than at the end of each billing cycle. The information derived from this data collection is personal in that it is easily linked to individuals and families, who may object to potentially invasive behavioral monitoring. For example, this information might allow a malicious hacker to accurately guess when a residence is empty or occupied.

The smart grid, in turn, is an early example of what will likely become the "smart home," as a growing array of devices helps consumers remotely monitor and control their daily activities. For instance, a refrigerator might report which food is fresh or in low supply, triggering an order to a grocery store. Motion detectors could provide information about who is in the home, allowing parents to remotely monitor the safety of their children. With the extensive ability to collect and use this sort of detailed information, security issues become paramount. Remote hackers could control the smart home and potentially access a massive amount of revealing and sensitive information. The issues for today's smart grid thus become a template for ongoing privacy and security concerns that will result from the shift to a smart home.

8. Direct Marketing

Direct marketing occurs when the seller directly contacts an individual, in contrast to marketing through mass media such as television or radio. Traditionally, there are two major privacy issues related to direct marketing: what information is collected and used by default, and what rights individuals have to change that default. The first issue concerns which records should be public and the limits on a company's internal use or resale of targeting information. The second issue includes opt-out measures taken by an individual to limit advertising ("please don't call my home any more") or opt-in measures to gain further information ("I do want to receive information about possible discounts on your product").

Direct marketing developments in the United States have allowed marketers access to a relatively wide range of public records. For instance, in the U.S., a person's name, address and telephone number are typically available through phone books and registered voter lists. The price of a family's home is usually available through real estate records. By contrast, most other countries have less extensive sets of public records.

Magazine subscription lists were an early, prominent example of direct marketing. Individuals who subscribed to one magazine (such as a fashion or sports magazine) would receive mail soliciting them to subscribe to similar magazines (other fashion or sports magazines). Over time, a self-regulatory system evolved in the United States, led primarily by the Direct Marketing Association, which established an opt-out system for consumers receiving mailings.[10] The next wave of direct marketing involved telephone calls to households. In the United States, a combination of self-regulation and government rules resulted in a company-by-company opt-out list that individuals could join. This expanded in 2004 with implementation of the National Do Not Call Registry, a regulation enforced by the Federal Trade Commission (FTC). By registering, individuals can opt out of receiving telemarketing phone calls. The Do Not Call rule contains an exception for political activities and nonprofit organizations, in order to uphold free speech rights.

With the rise of the Internet, policymakers engaged in extensive debate about how to both enable direct marketing and protect privacy. Enabling marketing was viewed as important in part to support the wide range of free content offered on the Internet. However, privacy concerns continued to surface as websites and companies with an Internet presence received and sometimes used detailed information about user surfing habits.

In 2000, a high-profile court case brought this matter to light. A leading online advertising network, DoubleClick, proposed to combine offline data about users with information collected by cookies set by DoubleClick's own network.[11] DoubleClick eventually agreed not to merge offline and online data. The decision also prompted the development of a self-regulatory code managed by the Network Advertising Initiative (NAI). The NAI code, for entities that adopt it, requires online advertising networks to provide an opt-out for many forms of online targeted advertising.[12]

With the continued spread of cookies and other online tracking mechanisms, marketing companies increased their use of targeted advertising to Internet and mobile users. These changes have led to new debates about protecting consumer privacy while supporting the Internet economy. The 2002 Privacy and Electronic Communications Directive (e-Privacy Directive) affirmed the right of individuals to place limits on direct marketing in the European Union.[13] The e-Privacy Directive was then amended in 2009. Sometimes called the "Cookie Directive," its revision placed stricter limits on online advertising than existed before.[14] Notably, it requires affirmative consent before cookies can be placed on an individual's computer. As of early 2012, national laws implementing the e-Privacy Directive are beginning to come into effect. There have been ongoing discussions about how to comply with the Directive while maintaining functionality of websites that use cookies.

In the United States, recent debates about targeted online advertising have focused mainly on the Do Not Track proposal by the FTC.[15] Proponents of the measure support Do Not Track as a commonsense update to the Do Not Call approach for telemarketing. It is unclear, however, how "tracking" is defined and what sorts of limits should be placed on advertising efforts. The Worldwide Web Consortium (W3C) is establishing standards to define Do Not Track, which may provide guidance on these issues. Beyond the technical issues about how standards should be defined, another controversy surrounds the extent to which Do Not Track would limit only use—the display of targeted ads to those who opt out—or, by contrast, would also limit the collection of information by websites and ad networks.

At a broad level, current issues about direct marketing illustrate the shift from historical broadcast-style marketing to a far more personalized advertising experience. Traditional television ads and billboards were designed for a wide audience, and advertisers received limited feedback about which advertising efforts were effective. Today, however, there is an increasing range of methods that advertisers can use to access information about potential consumers and, in turn, tailor their ads to individual consumer behavior. This personalization both provides individuals with more relevant advertising and affords advertisers a more efficient method of marketing. On the other hand, with personalization also come unprecedented amounts of information that can potentially be linked to the individual, raising privacy concerns. Ongoing changes in technology, such as the rapidly evolving smartphones and mobile marketing ecosystem, will continue to raise controversy and debate about how direct marketing will proceed, consistent with privacy protections.

9. Summary

This chapter has highlighted the possibility that specialized privacy rules and practices can apply to specific sectors, such as healthcare, finance, telecommunications, the Internet and the government. Privacy professionals should be alert to the possible existence of these specialized regimes. Other areas that may have specific rules include human resources, the energy market and marketing (such as limits on phone calls, e-mails, or direct mailings). The basic structure of fair information practices typically applies across these sectors, but the detailed rules and practices may vary.

Endnotes

1   Peter Tyson, "The Hippocratic Oath: Modern Version," WGBH Educational Foundation, 2001, www.pbs.org/wgbh/nova/body/hippocratic-oath-today.html.

2   Gramm–Leach–Bliley Act, 15 U.S.C. §§6801-6809.

3   Kojin jyoho no hogo ni kansuru horitsu [Act on the Protection of Personal Information], Law No. 57 of 2003, www.caa.go.jp/seikatsu/kojin/houritsu/050815houan.pdf. The English translation is available at www.caa.go.jp/seikatsu/kojin/foreign/act.pdf.

4   Between 1993 and 2009 the European Union was composed of three legal pillars. The European Community served as the first pillar, the Common Foreign and Security Policy as the second pillar, and the Cooperation in Justice and Home Affairs as the third pillar.

5   International Association for Human Resource Information Management (IHRIM) Code of Conduct, www.ihrim.org/Policies/CodeOfConduct.pdf.

6   www.ipc.on.ca/images/Resources/pbd-ont-smartgrid-casestudy.pdf.

7   CA Senate Bill 1476, www.leginfo.ca.gov/pub/09-10/bill/sen/sb_1451-1500/sb_1476_bill_20100929_chaptered.html.

8   http://eur-lex.europa.eu/LexUriServ/LexUriServ.do?uri=CELEX:52011DC0202:EN:HTML:NOT.

9   http://ec.europa.eu/justice/policies/privacy/docs/wpdocs/2011/wp183_en.pdf.

10 Since 1971, the Direct Marketing Association has offered DMAchoice (formerly known as the Mail Preference Service, or MPS), the official mail preference suppression service for the catalog marketing community. See www.dmachoice.org/.

11 In re DoubleClick Inc. Privacy Litigation, 154 F. Supp. 2d 497 (S.D.N.Y. 2001).

12 Opt Out of Behavioral Advertising, National Advertising Initiative, www.networkadvertising.org/managing/opt_out.asp. If NAI members wish to use sensitive information (government-issued ID numbers, precise real-time location information, financial and health information) for online behavioral advertising, the NAI code requires them to obtain consumer opt-in consent. Network Advertising Initiative Code of Conduct for Online Behavioral Advertising, §III.3(a)(iv), www.networkadvertising.org/networks/2008_NAI_Principles_PR_FINAL.pdf.

13 2002/58/EC, Directive of the European Parliament of the Council of 12 July 2002 concerning the processing of personal data and the protection of privacy in the electronic communications sector.

14 European Directive 2009/136, http://eur-lex.europa.eu/LexUriServ/LexUriServ.do?uri=OJ:L:2009:337:0011:0036:En:PDF.

15 Federal Trade Commission, "Protecting Consumer Privacy in an Era of Rapid Change: A Proposed Framework for Businesses and Policymakers" December 1, 2010, www.ftc.gov/os/2010/12/101201privacyreport.pdf.

CHAPTER FOUR

Information Security

Safeguarding Personal Information

1. Introduction to Information Security

The increasing interconnectivity of business today exposes information to a wide number of threats. **Information security (IS)** is the protection of information in order to prevent loss, unauthorized access or misuse. It is also the process of assessing threats and risks to information and the procedures and controls to preserve the information consistent with three key attributes:

1. **Confidentiality.** Access to data is limited to authorized parties.

2. **Integrity.** Assurance that the data is authentic and complete.

3. **Availability.** Knowledge that the data is accessible, as needed, by those who are authorized to access it.

Information security is achieved by implementing controls, which need to be monitored and reviewed, to ensure that organizational security objectives are met. It is vital to both public and private sector organizations.

Types of Security Controls

Security controls are mechanisms put in place to prevent, detect or correct a security incident. They can be classified in the following manner:

- **Physical controls**, *such as locks, security cameras, and fences*
- **Administrative controls**, *such as incident response procedures and training*
- **Technical controls**, *such as firewalls, antivirus software and access logs*

Information security is different from information privacy. Generally, information security is the protection of information, be it personal or other types of information, from unauthorized access, use and disclosure. Information privacy also concerns rules that govern the collection and handling of personal information. Despite this distinction, the two concepts are similar and overlap in certain respects. Information security is a necessary component of privacy protection—if security is breached, then privacy controls will not be effective. Information privacy and information security both concern the use, confidentiality and access to personal information. Information privacy, however, also involves the data subject's right to control the data, such as rights to notice and choice.

Figure 4-1: Privacy vs. Security

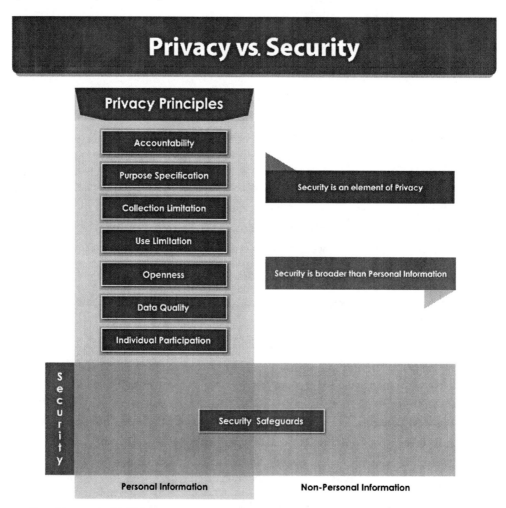

The table uses the OECD Privacy principles, which can be replaced with any set of privacy principles.

Used with permission from Nymity Inc.

Security requirements are derived from three main sources. First, requirements result from identifying and assessing the security threats to and vulnerabilities of the organization. Second, legal, regulatory and contractual obligations can help an organization define security requirements. Third, the organization's principles, policies and objectives will further inform an organization's security requirements.

After security threats, vulnerabilities and requirements have been identified, security controls must be implemented. The selection of these controls will depend on an organization's specific needs. For example, the security needs of a financial institution may be greater than those of an organization that does not handle sensitive personal information. Various types of security controls will be discussed in depth throughout this chapter.

When establishing and managing an information security program, consider these basic steps:

1. Define the scope and boundaries of the information security management system. This includes your security policy and overall program in terms of the business, organization, location, assets and technologies involved.

2. Define the security policy.

3. Define the risk assessment approach.

4. Identify, analyze and evaluate risks.

5. Identify and evaluate options for handling risks.

6. Select control objectives and controls for risks.

7. Obtain management approval or proposed residual risks.

8. Monitor and review the security program.

2. Information Identification and Assessment

An effective information security system begins with an assessment process. In general terms, this process evaluates the current state of the information technology (IT) infrastructure, including an inventory of all data assets and the identification of processes used for entering, changing and accessing the data in these systems. From a privacy perspective, assessment is an essential first step because privacy professionals cannot determine how secure a system is until they know what the system contains and how it operates.[1]

A thorough assessment can be quite complex and often involves many people across different departments, but it is important not to abbreviate the process. Without a thorough understanding of the IT infrastructure and the data control processes, any future attempts to increase security may be, at best, ineffective or, at worst, detrimental to the basic business functions of the organization. A good assessment will provide not only a technical schematic of the infrastructure and processes but also insight into how individuals actually use these systems on a day-to-day basis; it should provide a complete picture of how data systems operate in reality and not just theory.[2] While assessment is essentially backward-looking (i.e., determining how things have been done previously), monitoring provides current or real-time information about the system. Without monitoring, it is impossible to know what is occurring on the system on an ongoing basis.

Definitions of Risk, Threat and Vulnerability

According to the National Institute of Standards and Technology:

- *"Risk" is a measure of the extent to which an entity is threatened by a potential circumstance or event. It is typically a function of adverse impacts if the circumstance occurs and likelihood of occurrence.*
- *"Threat" is any circumstance or event with the potential to adversely impact organizational operations or assets—for example, malicious attacks or human/machine errors.*
- *"Vulnerability" is a weakness in an information system, system security procedures, internal controls or implementation that could be exploited by a threat source.*

The most common form of monitoring is system logs. System logs capture a current record of changes to the system and other important events. At a minimum, system logs need to record the presence of new and unauthorized accounts, the running of unauthorized programs and the access privileges of those operating on the system. It is also important that logs be checked regularly for gaps that may indicate they have been altered to conceal a security breach.[3] Logs should have some form of access control to prevent unauthorized tampering.

2.1 Risk Assessment Factors

To minimize risk to an information system, many factors need to be considered, managed and minimized to the best of an organization's abilities. One industry-standard risk assessment formula is:

$$Risk = Threat \; x \; Vulnerability \; x \; Expected \; Loss$$

Security metrics help evaluate the effectiveness of security policies, processes and products as well as calculate the risk and determine the value of reducing or mitigating the risk.

Some of the metrics that contribute to a risk/threat/vulnerability/loss matrix are the number of security breaches, the number of system outages and the number of lost information assets. Additional factors include the presence of software viruses and the use of investigations such as computer auditing and forensics (described further under "Incident Management" below).

- **Number of breaches.** A breach occurs when an attacker enters the organization's system, even if no information is altered or stolen. Low-level breaches can be common, but the essential feature is how well an organization reacts. Often, an initial breach can allow subsequent breaches to happen more easily. Therefore, the breach must be remedied as soon after detection as possible.

- **Number of outages.** An outage occurs when a component of the information system is taken offline as the result of an attack. Outages are a frightening—but not necessarily cataclysmic—outcome of a security breach. If an organization retains cached information, the users may never know that there has been an outage in the system.[4] At a much higher level, however, countries could be seriously affected if they were to become the successful target of a terrorist or nation-state attack to the power grid or other central system or utility. Both public and private security systems need to be in place and include an integrated plan for how to react should an outage occur on a massive scale.[5]

- **Unauthorized access.** This occurs when an individual who does not have proper authorization to view information does so. It may lead to improper modifications, disclosures or deletions.[6] This may apply to e-mail, databases or confidential reports. Often, unauthorized access may be detected by noting unusual access patterns to a system.[7]

- **Lost assets.** Losses can be in the form of money or data, occurring through theft, a breach or improper disposal techniques.

- **Software viruses.** Receipt of e-mails and visits to malicious websites are two of the most common ways to become infected with a virus.

- **Investigations.** An organization's audit and monitoring controls aid an investigation. The administrator should be able to work backwards through the logs, reports and forensics to determine the nature and extent of the attack. The investigation should occur both during and after the attack to ensure the shortest response time and least data loss.

3. Security Policy and Standards

After assessing existing security vulnerabilities, organizations should adopt and implement an information security policy that fits with its short-term and long-term objectives. In selecting and drafting a policy, many factors must be considered, some of which may be at odds with one another. For example, a financial institution may require a security policy that is rigorous enough to meet regulatory and legal requirements but also easy for new employees to use before thorough training can be completed. Organizations must therefore make careful, big-picture considerations before selecting a security policy, to avoid conflicts with other organizational objectives. The policy should also be crafted in a way that anticipates future security issues the organization may encounter.

In adopting a security policy, consideration should also be given to existing information security standards. The International Organization for Standardization (ISO) is a nongovernmental organization that promulgates and publishes business standards to promote quality control across the globe. The ISO network consists of over 160 member countries and representatives from national standards organizations. It provides consistent product and process evaluation, implementation, monitoring, and audit and maintenance procedures. These internationally recognized standards are used in both the public and private sectors.

For information security, ISO has issued two main standards. ISO 27001 applies to information security management. It is the common model for implementing and operating an information security management system, and its requirements are mandatory. It provides a comprehensive set of controls comprising international best practices for information security management.

ISO 27002 outlines international best practices for information security techniques and provides optional guidelines for implementing the requirements of ISO 27001. ISO 27002 was originally named ISO 17799, which was adopted from BS 7799-1, a British security standard. ISO 17799 was revised and reissued during 2005, and then renamed ISO 27002 in 2007.

This standard defines an overarching security framework consisting of 133 specific controls organized around 39 control objectives. The 11 security clauses of ISO 27002 each have categories of controls and implementation guidance. These security clauses are security policy; organization of information security; asset management; access and control; compliance; human resources security; physical and environmental security; information systems acquisition, development and maintenance; communications and operation management; business continuity management; and information security incident management. These information standards are useful to consult in designing a policy for your organization.

4. Security Organization

Every organization should have a defined information security management review system, although the complexity of the system will depend on the size of the organization. For effective information security coordination, a team in a large organization should consist of cross-functional groups, including managers, users, administrators, developers, auditors, security personnel and others. IS management should ensure that employees have adequate knowledge and experience to manage the operation and protection of all computer systems. Hiring only qualified professionals, such as those certified in information systems security (CISSP), information management (CISM) and/or information auditing (CISA), can be a prudent way to ensure an objective, validated standard of expertise. Additionally, organizations should provide for ongoing training in technologies, policies and methods in order to keep the entire information security team knowledgeable and current.

IT Roles and Responsibilities

To maintain security within an organization, roles and responsibilities must be clearly understood.

Chief Executive Officer and Executive Committee
- *Oversee overall corporate security strategy*
- *Lead by example and sponsor adoption of security*

Chief Security Officer
- *Sets security strategy and policies*
- *Facilitates the implementation of security controls*
- *Undertakes security risk assessments*
- *Designs risk management strategy*
- *Coordinates independent audits*

Security Personnel

- *Implement, audit, enforce and assess compliance*
- *Advise and validate security designs and maintenance*
- *Keep abreast of new security developments (vulnerabilities, exploits, patches, etc.)*
- *Communicate policies, programs and training*
- *Monitor for security incidents*
- *Respond to security breaches*

Outsourced Security Functions

- *Supplement internal security personnel*
- *Should be overseen by internal security personnel*

Managers and Employees

- *Implement security controls*
- *Report security vulnerabilities and breaches*
- *Maintain awareness of security in action*

The security department should develop comprehensive security policies and procedures and communicate these to the organization as a whole—not just the immediate privacy and security groups concerned. These policies should incorporate industry standard best practices such as those espoused by the National Institute of Standards in Technology in the United States, the IT Governance Institute's Control Objectives for Information and Related Technology, and the ISO standards 17799, 27001 and 27002.

It is important that the security department have a role in overseeing system administration groups when it comes to validating and communicating system maintenance. Regular system maintenance is one of the simplest and most important security functions. Security patches come out often for operating systems and applications, and it is important to apply these patches promptly.[8] However, system administrators can be reluctant to make changes to a system because they view their role more as ensuring system uptime than security. Since patches can sometimes create system instability, administrators may wait as long as possible to apply them.

Ultimately, security is about people—not technology. The information security department should help its organization understand that security is everyone's job. With that in mind, security training must become an integral part of the knowledge base for the many employees who work with the IT systems.

Employees should be trained to recognize security incidents and know the process for reporting them (covered in more detail in "Incident Management" below). Employees should know and be expected to follow security policies and procedures. Finally, employees should understand essential security basics such as not sharing passwords, not talking business in public and avoiding social engineering. IS management systems should require legally enforceable terms for nondisclosure and protection of confidential information. Employees should also be familiar with regulated requirements, policies, standards and procedures that affect their industry. Where there is high employee turnover or practical limits on available training, the IT system itself should be robust against mistakes or intentional but unauthorized access by the untrained employees. Finally, periodic independent reviews of the organization's information security posture should be made.

Information Technology Training

Technology alone cannot provide information security—education and awareness among employees are key. Ensure that all employees understand:

- *The value of security and the importance of recognizing and reporting incidents*
- *Their roles and responsibilities in fulfilling their security responsibilities*
- *Security policies and procedures, including password protection, information sensitivity and information protection*
- *Basic security issues such as virus, hacking and social engineering*
- *The importance of compliance with legal/regulatory requirements*

---

5. Security Infrastructure

Infrastructure requiring protection includes computer and network hardware, network systems and computer platforms.

5.1 Computer Hardware

Knowledge of the computer hardware and the physical IT infrastructure are important elements of information security. One must understand where the information physically resides on a network before the information can be secured. For example, if a person has physical access to a server computer's data drives, hubs, routers, external ports or any other accessible parts of the computer, many security controls are easily subverted. Controlling physical access to network switching and routing devices is important in this context, as will be discussed further below.[9]

A wide variety of computer hardware devices is in use at any given moment in an average-sized organization. These include mainframe computers, server computers, network computers, desktop computers, laptop computers, mobile devices (such as smartphones and tablets) and portable storage media (such as auxiliary data devices or "flash" drives). Each of these hardware devices has the ability to receive, store and accept access to personal information. Yet as the size, power, capacity and extensibility of the hardware increases, the levels of control and protection of the personal information are further challenged.

Laptop and tablet computers offer two compelling examples. Both pose two distinct types of information security problems.

The first involves information legitimately stored on these devices. While it is often convenient to keep information such as contacts, addresses and personal schedules on a smartphone or tablet, the very mobility of the device is also its greatest security weakness. Mobile devices are easily lost or stolen, making any information stored on the device susceptible to loss or abuse. If information is stored on a mobile or handheld device, proper practice is often to encrypt the data so that, if lost or stolen, the data would remain inaccessible.

The second problem involves data theft. As handheld devices become more sophisticated, they pose a greater threat to information security. One risk is that mobile phones, tablet computers and similar handheld mass storage devices can be easily modified so that when connected to any machine equipped with a USB data port, they automatically copy the contents of the connected hard drive.[10] Once the storage device is detected, the operating system of the hard drive may automatically attempt to mount the drive, which would allow a data thief to bypass many of the standard system security controls. While not as sophisticated, portable storage media (such as the popular "flash" memory drives, memory sticks or "thumb" drives) pose a similar threat. These devices can store gigabytes of data on digital media smaller than a stick of gum. This sort of availability and simplicity offers an inviting opportunity for a hacker or exploit artist. A data thief can easily use a flash drive to remove sensitive information without detection.[11]

An organization should thus consider when to disable flash drives, as well as downloads to mobile devices more generally. Desktop workstations (office personal computers) pose particular risks because it is difficult for IT professionals to control access to the information stored on them. This type of risk can be the rationale for not using mass storage devices or other peripherals connected to them, as well as for installing auditing systems to deter and detect unauthorized mass downloads of sensitive data.

5.2 Network Hardware

Network hardware typically refers to equipment such as routers, switches, gateways and access points that facilitate the use and management of a computer network. These systems are almost always managed by networking systems professionals. Network hardware is extremely powerful and is the linchpin of network security. If one of these devices is compromised, it is easy for an attacker to gain access to the entire network. These devices have therefore been designed with security in mind, and a good network engineer can use them to enhance data security.

Network servers are centralized computers that may contain business information accessible to many users, often simultaneously. These machines are the heart of business functionality and the key to data flows across an organization as well as to outside partners and users. Information security starts with server security. An organization's network architecture needs to be designed such that server operating systems are stripped of nonessential services and "hardened" for security.

5.3 Network Systems

Two broad categories of network systems are local and wide area networks.

- **Local area networks (LANs)** exist within an operational facility, are considered within local operational control and are relatively easy to manage.

- **Wide area networks (WANs)** may involve coordination between several groups, are considered outside of local operational control and are relatively difficult to manage.

Ethernet is the most common type of LAN connection. It is based on a broadcast model and trusts the responses it receives. Thus, Ethernet has some inherent security vulnerabilities related to reliability, interception and spoofing (receiving false inputs). However, with proper network design and management, Ethernet can be made very safe.[12] Optical connections are increasingly common in connecting WANs. Optical networks use complex light wave patterns to transmit information rather than electrical impulses. The protocols used over optical networks (such as ATM, FDDI and HPPI) are more modern and more robust, and incorporate much more security than Ethernet.

The following network systems also need to be managed in order to ensure effective information security.

- **Internet.** Managing and securing information accessible to the Internet is extremely important (and is discussed further in Chapter 5, "Online Privacy"). Since it is difficult, if not impossible, to completely secure any Internet-connected machine, privacy professionals with sensitive information can consider creating networks that are separate from Internet-connected networks. For example, the U.S. Department of Defense maintains three physically separate networks: (1) an Internet-connected network, (2) a general internal network, and (3) a classified data network. No machine or device is allowed to connect to more than one of these networks at any time, creating an "air gap"—a barrier against gaining access from one network to another. While this practice enhances information security, physical separation from the Internet may not be feasible in a particular business environment.

- **The cloud.** Securing information stored on the cloud (discussed further in Chapter 5) can be challenging. Though the concept of cloud computing is still evolving, most definitions include common components of on-demand accessibility, scalability and secure access from almost any location. When data is stored on the cloud, it is subject to security risks unique to the cloud environment. Therefore, data stored on the cloud must be afforded adequate protection, which will differ depending on the classification of the information and the organization's security needs.

- **Intranet.** An intranet refers to a private computer network or group of private computer networks within an organization. It is used to facilitate communication and exchange of information between users (employees) or workgroups. An intranet functions and looks like a private version of the Internet; however, it is accessible only to the organization's members or others with appropriate authorization. Typically, a network gateway and firewall protect an intranet from unauthorized access.

- **Extranet.** Many businesses find it both practical and expedient to share internal information, directly and in real time, with external business partners, vendors, customers and/or subsidiary businesses. An extranet is just such a network system formed through the connection of two or more corporate intranets. These external networks create inherent security risks, while often also meeting important organizational goals. An extranet opens a back door into the internal network and provides a third party with a level of trust. Although these risks cannot be eliminated, they can be assessed, managed and mitigated.[13] The foundation of this management is a thorough and detailed e-business contract that specifies who may access data, what data will be accessed and what security controls the partner has in place. The contract should also detail how shared devices will be managed, procedures for cooperating with technical staff in the event of problems and escalation procedures for resolving difficult technical problems.

- **Private branch exchange (PBX).** Standard telecommunications equipment is often underprotected in comparison to more advanced networking systems. Most office telephone systems are controlled by a private branch exchange (PBX) system. These systems control telephone interactions, store voicemails, and perform many other functions related to telephony. PBX systems are often connected to the internal network for management and monitoring and many run on standard servers. However, infiltration and manipulation of a company's telephone system can pose serious information security risks. Therefore, steps should be taken to protect PBX systems and telecommunications equipment.

- **Remote access connectivity.** Remote access is an important business capability but it also introduces pronounced security risks. Mobile connectivity should generally be managed through a **virtual private network** (VPN), a system that incorporates authentication and encryption schemes in order to create a secure connection to an organizational LAN that is made available to authorized users over the Internet.[14] This type of connectivity is most familiar to telecommuters who log on to corporate networks from a home office or remote location through a secure connection.

- **Mobile and wireless network connectivity.** These are accomplished through software protocols that travel over standard radio waves and negotiate wireless connections among laptops, other mobile devices and landline networks. Often referred to as "wireless fidelity" or "Wi-Fi," the radio waves that carry the wireless data are relatively easy to intercept and emulate and thus pose a number of information security threats. The first is data interception, where the attacker can understand the content of the communications. This risk can be managed through the use of an encrypted network signal.

The second problem is data emulation, which is more difficult to combat. In this scenario, certain devices can imitate a wireless base transceiver and hijack a network session, leading to the interception of passwords and other sensitive information that may pass over the network during the session. Technologies with stronger controls are being developed to combat this risk, but having a mobile device with properly configured network settings can be a significant first step in reducing the scope of this risk before stronger, more robust solutions are publicly available.

- **Voice over Internet protocol (VoIP).** VoIP allows telephone calls to be made over a private WAN or the Internet itself. Skype is a well-known example. VoIP poses the same risk as network-connected PBX systems but also poses the additional risk of data interception when such data travels over an unsecured connection. Because VoIP faces the same risk as Internet connections generally, VoIP functionality should be encrypted where possible, and equipment can be locked down, placed behind firewalls, patched against vulnerabilities and monitored with intrusion-detection systems in much the same way as a WAN (see above).

- **Electronic mail.** By default, e-mail has historically been sent over the network in easy-to-read, unencrypted form. Anyone who has access to the network traffic then has the ability to see the data contained in a text e-mail. The electronic message can easily be read in transit, and potentially changed and then sent on to its intended recipient without the recipient's being aware of any alteration. E-mail encryption at either the network or application layer, or both, can prevent either of these eventualities, and webmail services increasingly are encrypted by default. However, encryption by itself does not ensure that the person sending the mail is the person he/she claims to be. This raises the issue of nonrepudiation, or the risk that the sender may deny (repudiate) having sent the message. Public keys and digital signatures can be used to solve this problem and are discussed in Sections 8.3 and 8.4.[15]

5.4 Computer Platforms

Computer platforms can be grouped into three general categories: mainframe, server, and desktop and smaller computers.

- **Mainframe computers.** Many enterprises, especially banks and government agencies, continue to rely on mainframe computers as a key part of their IT infrastructure. Mainframes are very large computing hardware installations, hailing from the very earliest days of information technology, and are generally housed within a physically secure mainframe building area. They present challenges from an information security perspective by virtue of their sheer size and the scope of data they contain and process. System administrators, intent on other organizational goals, may be reluctant to make changes on these legacy machines and there can be correspondingly large security holes. The impact of any exploitation or breach of these machines can be enormous due to the large data sets typically processed.

- **Server computers.** Typically smaller and less powerful than mainframes, server computers satisfy many of the same enterprise functions because they can be linked to other servers across a network. By design, servers are broadly distributed and can be physically located anywhere—not just within the same facility but at remote sites. However, such distribution of tasks makes these machines more difficult to secure both logically and physically. Virtual server technology now allows the creation of multiple "virtual" environments on one server platform, potentially consolidating large amounts of disparate data in one location.

- **Desktop and other personal computers.** As discussed above, desktops, laptops, smartphones and other devices operated by people outside of an IT department are increasingly powerful and able to store large amounts of information. However, for security purposes, no business-critical information should exclusively be stored on such a device. Business-critical information should be managed in a centralized manner where it can be secured, backed up and included in a disaster recovery plan.

6. Security Controls

Security controls are the actual processes used to ensure the security of an information system. It is imperative that these controls be in place and function as intended. It is also important that a control monitoring process be set up to provide prompt notification in the event that any of the controls fails.

Generally, there are three main types of information security controls:

1. **Preventive** security controls are intended to stop incidents before they can impact operations. Preventive controls are the most common and include password verifiers and firewall systems, among other approaches.

2. **Detective** security controls are generally more complex than preventive controls. Detective controls are aware of normal operations and look for system anomalies such as unusual activities or events. Detective controls ideally are dynamic and able to watch for new and previously unknown security threats. Detective security controls most commonly come in the form of intrusion detection systems (IDS), which are defined later in this chapter.

3. **Corrective** security controls can take automatic actions to manage or mitigate a security threat after a preventive or detective control has provided an alert about that threat. Corrective controls are generally integrated into other controls, such as intrusion prevention systems (IPS), which are defined later in this chapter.

One can also consider each of these controls as hybrids of procedure and technology. Each approach above includes elements of established process to anticipate or prevent errors, irregularities or unauthorized access. In addition, each approach includes the hardware and software technologies required to maintain technical security. These can include system diagnostic devices, software patches and other tools. Finally, these controls can include facets of physical security such as facility oversight or environmental management.

6.1 Encryption and Decryption

Encryption is an important category of techniques for ensuring effective system security and preventing unauthorized access to private information: it can encode the data sent from one computer to another ("encryption in communication") or encode data stored locally ("encryption at rest"). Decryption is the function used to reverse the encryption of information and reveal it in plain text. Encryption is a good means of ensuring confidentiality but not authentication. Thus, the fact that a message is encrypted does not verify that the person who claims to have sent the message is the true sender. Digital signatures are often used to address this problem and are covered in Section 8.4.[16] Encryption is further discussed in Section 8 of this chapter.

> **Encryption**
>
> *Encryption is the process of obscuring information, often through the use of a cryptographic scheme, to make the data unreadable without special knowledge (e.g., the use of code keys).*

7. Information Asset Management

Information security systems must be designed and implemented with the dual purpose of providing access to the end user while protecting the data from other end users.[17] Misuse of systems by authorized users is a very common cause of data loss and data compromise in the marketplace today. Users should be provided access only to data appropriate for their specific job.[18] All high-level access (e.g., root or administrator-level privileges) should be reserved for technical or security professionals. A privacy professional must always work with the user in mind, both to keep the user's system secure and to secure the system from the user.[19]

As discussed, the first step in protecting information is to understand what data your organization holds, and who—both within and outside the organization—owns such data. This means not only identifying what the information is but also where the information is physically located. Once the information is identified, it is also important to create an asset-tracking process so that machines containing personal information can be operated, repaired, maintained, reused and retired securely. Again, this tracking principle applies to information that is owned by the organization as well as information that is owned by others, but used by the organization.

7.1 Retention of Records

Retaining sensitive data—including personal information—is imperative for a variety of reasons, including for tax, audit, and other business and legal purposes. Aside from the obvious concerns about organizational integrity, there are business and legal factors that must be considered.

Retention schedules should address record types (level of sensitivity) and retention periods (duration of storage) and should be based on demonstrated business needs as well as any applicable regulatory requirements. Process controls should be implemented that protect essential data from loss, falsification or inadvertent destruction. In many jurisdictions there are special destruction considerations to ensure personal information is not destroyed after a data subject, government agency or other access request has been received.

7.2 Duplication and Destruction of Records

Duplicates of important records should be maintained in case one copy is displaced or lost entirely. However, maintaining multiple sets of sensitive data compounds the difficulty of keeping such data private. These factors must all be weighed when evaluating the costs and benefits of maintaining multiple record copies.

Once it is determined that personal information is no longer needed, it should be anonymized or securely destroyed. While paper records are easily shredded and disposed of, electronic records are more difficult to completely eliminate. Even when electronic records are deleted from a computer system's file directory, the record itself is not necessarily eliminated and the "deleted" data might be recoverable.[20] Computer operating systems generally function much like the traditional library card catalog: when a new file is created, the operating system creates a record showing where the file is located on the drive. When the file is "deleted," the operating system deletes the record showing the old file location and then indicates that the physical space is free to accommodate a new file. However, the file itself is not deleted, though it eventually may be overwritten with new data. Yet even in that case, the old data may still be accessible using forensic techniques.

Traditional computer hard drives work by using a magnet to change the polarity of charged particles on the surface of the magnetic disc. This process is inexact at the atomic level, so that even after the drive head writes new data in an area, a magnetic "shadow" of the previous data may remain. For example, security experts were able to recover readable sensitive information off the hard drives purchased from resellers on eBay using readily available software even after the drives had been reformatted and overwritten many times.[21] From 158 drives, the team recovered 5,000 credit card numbers, and one drive, apparently from an ATM machine, contained a year's worth of transactions, including account numbers and other sensitive bank information. More modern solid state drives, which are often used in high-performance transaction processing systems and typically process personal information, can also retain data after being deleted by the operating system.

Persons implementing information security thus need to understand the data structures of computer operating systems, the physical properties of computer hard drives and best practices for protecting data across both systems and drives.

7.3 Information Classification

Information directories and the records they contain may be quantified according to their value to the organization, as well as by ownership, how critical such information is to the operations of the organization and how sensitive it is according to applicable laws. Generally speaking, the higher the value of the information and its sensitivity, the greater the security required. For example, an employee directory may not be as highly valued as a customer database that includes sensitive personal information—depending on the country within which the organization operates and the corresponding legal requirements in that jurisdiction regarding acquisition, storage, use and/or disclosure of personal information. Once a value has been given to the information asset, then a classification can be established and a corresponding security level can be identified and implemented.

Information Asset Classification

Information should be protected in accordance with the value of the asset—the higher the value, the greater the security needed.

Asset value should be evaluated based on:

- *Sensitivity and confidentiality*
- *Potential liability*
- *Intelligence value*
- *Criticality to the business*

Effective risk management balances the potential for loss with the cost of security protection and management.

An information classification scheme provides the basis for managing access to, and protection of, information assets as well as for establishing a clear understanding of the relative sensitivity of the information. Asset value can be evaluated based on a number of factors, including confidentiality, potential liability, intelligence value (for government or business) and criticality to the organization. Effective information security—and risk management generally—balances the potential for loss of these assets with the cost of their security protection and management.

Three of the most common information classification levels are confidential, sensitive and public:

- **Confidential** information, if disclosed, would cause the business to be seriously compromised or outright fail (e.g., customer databases that include a large amount of sensitive personal information). This class of information should remain highly secure and private.

- **Sensitive** data is important business information that is intended for internal use only (e.g., company contact directories, strategic business plans or sales revenue forecasts) and should remain secure.

- **Public** information may be safely shared with the public at large (e.g., marketing materials or a company's address—though in some cases, the latter is considered sensitive for security purposes).

7.4 Outsourcing IT Functions

Many organizations engage in the collection and analysis of data or other IT functions. This can be a complicated, costly and time-consuming process. Your organization may elect to outsource these functions to an outside vendor or choose to sell the collected information to a third party.

While organizations generally ensure that outsourcing will function and produce a quality work product, they often do less to guarantee that outsourced data will remain secure. Even if IT systems are outsourced, the management and security of these systems must remain subject to effective oversight by internal personnel.[22] Your organization must also ensure the responsibility and security of data and IT functions once they are in the hands of a contractor or vendor. Thus, the claims in your security policy should hold true for any third parties that you work with. An organization should make certain that the service provider has sufficient security controls in place.

As discussed in Chapter 1, the security requirements of an organization that is engaging in outsourcing should be addressed in a contract that all parties agree on. This contract should include:

- Security roles and responsibilities
- Requirements for information protection in order to achieve levels of security with the third party that are equivalent to those of the organization
- Information ownership and appropriate use
- Physical and logical access controls
- Security control testing of the third party
- Continuity of services in the event of a disaster
- An incident coordination process
- The right to conduct audits
- A clear statement of respective liabilities

In addition to the agreement initiating the data relationship, sound operational practices should be implemented and supported by the underlying agreement. For example, one U.S. insurance company that outsources work to India has the following security procedures in place for the outsourced employees:[23]

- Employees and their belongings are subject to search when arriving and leaving the workplace.
- Cell phones are checked in and held until the day is over.
- Papers are shredded on a daily basis.
- Computer security prevents files from being moved or copied.
- Phone privileges are limited to calls to the help desk.
- The Internet and e-mail are similarly "locked down."

Again, effective business contracts with liability clauses are both advisable and necessary. Vendors ought to use the security controls discussed in this chapter and they should be reviewed by the contracting organization before entering into a contract. The contracting organization's information security department can further assist with assessment of these controls.

8. Access Control

Access by an individual employee to an organization's information systems should be tied to the role the employee plays, and policies for access may require further management approval at the departmental (IS/IT), operational (CIO/CTO) and, if necessary, executive (CEO) levels of the organization.

No employee should have greater information access than is necessary to capably perform his or her job function.

These types of precautions are known as "role-based access controls." They are built on three basic security principles:

1. **Segregation of duties.** Responsibility for the processing of information should be divided so that no individual acting alone can compromise the system. This is highly effective for security but can be costly and labor intensive.

2. **Least privilege.** Access is granted on the basis of the lowest possible level of access required to perform the function. Application of this principle limits the damage that can result from accident, error or unauthorized use of an information system.

3. **Need to know or access.** Access is based on the legitimate basis of a person or organization to know, access or possess specific information that is critical to the performance of an authorized, assigned mission.

Most commonly, job role/responsibility and executive clearance are the measures that determine the level of access control for a particular employee. In addition, individual system access accounts are necessary to ensure system accountability. The alternative—a shared or group account—is essentially anonymous and poses acute security risks. Organizations must know who is accessing information and when—down to each individual and each data element level. This keeps end users—whether employees, partners, suppliers or customers—accountable and facilitates quicker and easier identification when an account is compromised.

Nonrepudiation is the ability to ensure that neither the originator nor the receiver can dispute the validity of a transaction or access request. An independent verification takes place that allows the sender's identity to be verified, typically by a third party, and also allows the sender to know that the intended recipient of the message actually received it. Nonrepudiation of origin proves that data has been sent and nonrepudiation of delivery proves that the data has been received.

8.1 Authentication

Once individual access accounts have been identified, approved and established, information security professionals employ methods of authentication and authorization to monitor access and thus ensure system security over time.

Authentication identifies an individual account user based on one or more of the following:

- **What you know**—a password, for example, or answers to "secret" questions known to the user and the IT system, but not to others. Such questions should be "out of wallet"—not knowable even if an outsider gains access to the information in a user's wallet.

- **What you have**, such as a key or identity card. Many virtual private networks use a "key fob" or virtual token that cryptographically generates a new access code many times an hour, and synchronizes the code between the user and the server.
- **Who you are**, from the simple (someone recognizes your face) to more complex biometric systems, relying on fingerprints, voice recording, iris or retinal scans, etc.

Multifactor authentication schemes use two or more of the above types of credential. For instance, a password might be accompanied by one or more of the following:

- **Passcard:** An identity instrument that can range from a magnetic strip (similar to a credit card) to a more sophisticated device embedded with computer chips.
- **Biometric:** A biological identifier such as a fingerprint, palmprint, voice scan, iris scan or other unique physiological attribute that can be identified and evaluated dynamically through an available technology.
- **Out of band:** Restricted access to a website or hardware device that requires both a password and a one-time code sent over another channel, such as a text to a cellphone.

A two-factor process will typically combine what you know (for example, a username and password) with what you have (for example, a token that generates a one-time password), and check each before authenticating the access request.

8.2 Password Management

The most basic level of end user authentication is a password scheme—although such schemes can become complex. A password when used alone is an example of **"one-factor" authentication**, which relies on one input (the password sequence) to validate the end user.

Administrative passwords that allow broad access to information systems are particularly crucial to protect. In addition, system administrators should keep different passwords for their personal accounts and administrative privileges.

These are some of the industry-standard password conventions in use today:

- System passwords should be independently assigned and used (not shared).
- Blank-field passwords should never be used/allowed.
- Passwords should contain at least eight characters (if the system supports such length; if not, then as many characters as the system does support).
- A combination of upper- and lowercase letters, numbers, and at least one special character should be used in composing the password.
- Passwords should be actively cycled at least once every 30 days; existing passwords should be retired and replaced with new passwords.
- Inactive accounts or accounts of departed or terminated employees should be disabled completely.
- Password schemes should not be associated with anything that may be broadly familiar to the individual or others at the organization such as nicknames, pet names or known interests such as a favorite sports team.

- Common dictionary words, a well-known string of numbers or birthdates should be avoided in any password scheme.

Repeating or reusing existing passwords does not offer a viable alternative since a previous password can become compromised. However, maintaining a strong password scheme is often difficult because the more complex the password, the more difficult it often is for end users to memorize it and use it safely. When password aging is added to the complexity requirement, users will generally resort to writing down passwords or storing them in some other insecure manner.

Though passwords should never be stored in any location that is within plain view of a casual observer (both virtually and physically), sometimes this is not practicable. Password storage policies must be made with the understanding that access to a password is equivalent to access to the system itself.

The intent of a complex password scheme is to prevent "brute force" password attacks. These are exploits that attempt to undermine an individual password or group of passwords by running all possible word and number combinations against the system. Obviously, the simpler the password scheme, the more likely such an exploit will accurately determine the password and thus gain access to the system. With every extra character and character set in the password, the difficulty in guessing a password through a brute force attack or other exploit becomes exponentially more difficult.

Implementing a strong but user-friendly policy is an important part of ensuring a functional and effective one-factor (password-based) security framework.

8.3 Public Key Infrastructure (PKI)

PKI is a system of digital certificates, certificate authorities and other registration entities that verifies the validity of each party involved in an electronic transaction through the use of cryptographic (coded or encrypted) signatures. PKI enables users of insecure public networks (such as the Internet) to privately and securely authenticate with each other and to exchange electronic data and/or digital currency.

The term *PKI* represents a set of security ideals and the means to accomplish them. It can be applied to a number of different source technologies rather than any single technology.[24] PKI schemes permit a sender to create two unique tokens (identifiers) similar to the DSA algorithm described above:

1. A "public key" that allows anyone to encrypt data and send it securely to the recipient
2. A "private key" that allows the recipient to unlock the data signature and view the contents of the message in a readable format such as plain text

PKI implementations use encryption to try to guarantee the safety and reliability of data transmitted over an insecure network. An effective PKI implementation depends on factors such as a secure cryptosystem key length long enough to defeat brute force attacks, and effective implementation of the encryption system in the organization's IT infrastructure. Effective implementation can yield a number of security assurances:

- The data has not been altered or corrupted in transit.
- The source of the data is who or what it claims to be.

- The transmitted data has remained private and secure while in transit.
- The transmitted data may be introduced as evidence in a court of law.[25]

PKI implementations use public key encryption to fulfill these goals. The public key allows anyone to encrypt data and send it securely; the recipient then unlocks the data using his or her private key, the only key that will return the data to plain text.[26]

8.4 Digital Signatures

Digital signatures provide a means for ensuring the authenticity of an electronic document—whether an e-mail, text file, document, spreadsheet or image file. If anything is changed in the electronic document after the digital signature is attached, it also changes the value associated with the document, and this renders the signature invalid.

The Digital Signature Standard (DSS) is the certificate protocol most commonly used in connection with electronic documents. It is based on a type of public-key cryptography that uses the Digital Signature Algorithm (DSA) endorsed by many U.S. government agencies for the purpose of securing sensitive information. The DSA consists of a private key, known only by the originator of the document (the signer), plus a public key that is offered to recipients of the document.

The role of public and private keys differs for encryption and digital signatures. For encryption, the sender uses the recipient's public key when sending the message, and the recipient uses his or her private key to decode the message. For digital signatures, the sender first uses his or her own private key, and the recipient then uses the sender's public key to decode the message and determine that the signed document is authentic and has not been modified in transit.

8.5 Authorization

Authorization is the process of determining if the end user, once authenticated, is permitted to have access to the desired resource, such as the information asset or the information system containing the asset. Authorization criteria may be based on organizational role, job function, group or departmental membership, level of security clearance, applicable law, any combination of these factors or all of these factors. The process, when effective, validates that the person or entity requesting access is in fact who or what they claim to be.

Even with appropriate safeguards in place, on principle, no one person should have complete access to all business systems. The duties of systems and security administrators should be segregated. This provides accountability, oversight and mitigation of damages. Also, from a business continuity standpoint, no one person should be the only person who can perform any single, essential function. If that person is suddenly lost, then operations stop.

Changes in employee position, responsibility level or even employment status are some of the more common workplace events from an organizational perspective. System access levels need to be adjusted as an employee's role changes. Since these factors tend to be neglected, information systems must be reviewed periodically to ensure that accounts and access levels accurately reflect employment level and status. Where necessary, system access accounts should be deleted—particularly those of former employees.

9. Human Resources Information Security

The human resources department handles some of the organization's most sensitive data. Human resources databases are prime targets for identity thieves because of the easy access to identification numbers, date of birth and other personal information. For this reason, organizations should have some sort of written procedure that establishes administrative, technical and physical security of the data. Human resources roles in information security differ by stage of employment. To gain administrative security, the procedure should have a program definition and administration, manage workforce risks and provide thorough employee training. For technical security, the procedure should discuss the computer systems, networks, applications, access controls and encryption. Finally, for physical security, the procedure should describe the facilities, environmental safeguards and recovery process in the event of a disaster.

Prior to employment, security roles and responsibilities of those handling sensitive data should be clearly defined and documented according to the security policy, and should be clearly explained to new employees. Background verification checks should be completed on candidates for employment, contractors and third parties in accordance with classification of the information that will be accessed by these parties. During the hiring process, the terms and conditions of employment should be made clear to the potential employee.

During employment, management should require employees, contractors and third parties to apply security in accordance with established policies and procedures. Security awareness training should be given to employees based on job function. A formal disciplinary process should be established for any employee who violates the security policy, as such violations can lead to security breaches and loss or disclosure of information.

If there is a change or termination of employment, the responsibility for performing termination or change of employment should be clearly defined. Employees, contactors and third parties should return all of the organization's assets upon termination. Access rights should be removed upon termination or adjusted based on job function needs upon the change of employment.

If an organization chooses to outsource sensitive human resources data, it should establish a formal vendor security qualification protocol and audit against it to ensure that the data remains secure. The organization should also establish vendor contractual provisions such as mandating reasonable security, mandating notice of any security or confidentiality breach, and providing for audit rights, insurance and indemnification.

10. Physical and Environmental Information Security

Along with the technical and administrative measures used to ensure the security of an information system, it is also important to implement physical and environmental security measures. Theft of records, files or documents can have a crippling effect on your organization. If outside parties access your trade secrets, working models or other sensitive information, the viability of your organization could be at stake. Physical damage to facilities or equipment could also negatively affect your product or service, resulting in damage to consumer trust.

Types of physical controls vary, and each organization must complete an assessment to determine its needs. In-house security personnel and closed-circuit television can be used to monitor and inspect facilities, although such monitoring of employees may be subject to privacy limits in some countries. Alarm systems, key control management and reception areas can help restrict unauthorized access. Perimeter protection and barriers, such as fences and gates, can be used as security checkpoints.

In terms of physical location, sensitive information should not be stored in an area where the general public has access or where there is regular traffic of individuals who are not authorized to view such information. Critical equipment, cabling and other hardware should also be located away from potential hazards, such as fires, floods or other emergencies. Other general controls may also be necessary, such as processes for maintaining equipment, or for removing and disposing of equipment from your organization's facilities.

Laptop and mobile devices provide useful and common examples of the need for physical security. Without adequate physical protection, these devices are subject to theft or damage. Your organization may end up with a data breach through physical or system losses. Thus, it is important to use physical controls to mitigate these risks.

11. Intrusion Detection and Prevention

Based on the premise that prevention is the best possible cure, information security professionals strive to prevent any unauthorized access to data assets from occurring. This is accomplished through a variety of means, from modest hardware and software implementations (such as firewalls and antivirus solution suites) to more intricate methods of encrypting data while stored (such as the examples of public key encryption described elsewhere in this chapter).

Some of the most dangerous system vulnerabilities are the simplest. For example, an empty, logged-on workstation is the equivalent of an openly available user ID and password. Desktops should be configured to time-out after a certain period of inactivity and revert to a locked screensaver or other automated mechanism that prevents unauthorized access while the workstation user is away.

Improper Internet and e-mail use also offers an easy way for users to create network vulnerabilities. Incoming and outgoing e-mail should be scanned for viruses, suspect documents and executable software attachments such as spyware or adware applications.

Antivirus solutions offer a straightforward and relatively easy-to-implement protection against system intrusions of the software variety. Virus programs developed and deployed by "hackers" and other exploit artists from inside or outside the organization are often used to create specific vulnerabilities in the organization's network systems. These include "back doors" that allow immediate and open access as well as "Trojan" programs that masquerade as benign code but in fact become active later to allow unauthorized access to the network.

Other viruses may contain "keyloggers" that record everything that is typed into a computer through a keyboard or other input device (personal information that may include names, user

IDs, passwords and other data). The keylogger program monitors and records this data and transmits it back to the hacker.

Antivirus protection can be deployed against these system intrusions in several ways. The easiest is maintaining a centralized mail server with antivirus capabilities that scan incoming and outgoing messages. A more ambitious antivirus method scans all incoming data for virus signatures in the data streams, including the often-large attachments to e-mail.[27] If there is a large volume of network traffic, the machines handling the latter approach must have a large capacity to make this solution effective without slowing down network operations.

Firewalls are generally used as a means of protecting internal networks from unauthorized external access. A firewall is a software program that resides at the network router or server level and is configured with a policy that allows only certain types of traffic to access the network. Firewall policies can be very detailed and can be designated based on user, type of use, machine, time of day and/or application variety, among a multitude of other factors. The more specific the policy the more security it can provide—but also the more difficult the firewall is to manage and maintain.

Technical measures should be used to block access to potentially dangerous sites (e.g., hacker, gambling and pornographic sites often contain browser exploit code). These systems should also articulate clear use policies on e-mail and Internet access, and these policies should be consistent with the organizational security philosophy described in the employee manual or privacy policy.

11.1 Perimeter Controls

Information security professionals in general manage technologies and processes that are designed to secure an entire network environment by preventing penetration from the outside. This is called "controlling the perimeter" of the network. The different methods include:

- Network and host-based firewalls
- "Malware" (bad software) detection and antivirus application suites
- Access control lists (with antispoofing) that reside on networks
- Host and network-based intrusion detection systems (IDS)
- Host and network-based intrusion prevention systems (IPS)
- Connection encryption schemes such as virtual private networks (VPN), secure sockets layer (SSL) and Internet protocol security (IPSEC) protocols
- Strong user, e-mail and device encryption

Antivirus, firewall and encryption-based solutions have already been addressed in this chapter. The web-based security protocol of SSL is defined in Chapter 5.

11.2 Security Monitoring

Information security professionals can monitor the success of IDS, IPS and other perimeter controls through the use and analysis of log files. These are essentially "event reports" that are generated automatically based on the originating system, computer, software application or software tool.

Many computer operating systems, such as UNIX, Linux and Windows, record natural as well as suspect events ("anomalies") in any one or all of three different log types: application logs, system logs and security logs.

- The **application log** contains events logged by applications or programs. For example, a database program might record a file error in the application log. The program developer decides which events to record.

- The **system log** contains events logged by the operating system components. For example, the failure of a driver or other system component to load during startup is recorded in the system log. The event types logged by system components are predetermined for the operating system.

- The **security log** can record security events, such as valid and invalid logon attempts, as well as events related to resource use, such as creating, opening or deleting files. An administrator can specify what events are recorded in the security log. For example, if you have enabled logon auditing, attempts to log on to the system are recorded in the security log.[28]

12. External Threat Management

Threats to an information system can take many different forms and arrive through different channels—external and internal. The Internet poses a significant danger to any organization and remains a continued threat source with its preponderance of software viruses, spyware applications, phishing exploits and unsolicited e-mail ("spam").

One of the greatest security threats to an organization originates from inside. While much of security is aimed outward to protect against attacks from the public, many businesses fail to design their information security systems and policies to protect against an internal compromise. Data loss caused intentionally or inadvertently is still data loss—irrespective of source.

12.1 Exploit Tools

As acute as internal threats can be to an organization's data assets, external threats remain quite real. One reason is the easy availability of automated exploit tools: the largely homemade software programs that hackers develop and openly exchange with other exploit artists. They deploy these programs against information systems in various combinations, in both individual and combined attacks, with relative abandon and ruthless frequency.

Automated exploit tools are easily accessible but, luckily, are also recognizable and relatively easy to defend against. Typically, these exploit tools are developed by sophisticated hackers to maximize or take advantage of a known and common vulnerability in a particular system. However, since the vulnerability is common (i.e., widely known), software patches (fixes) from legitimate software developers usually become rapidly and widely available close to the time the exploit tool is distributed. Thus, for a prepared and vigilant security administrator, exploit tools usually pose minimal threat. By contrast, a slow response to vulnerabilities leaves a system vulnerable to "script kiddies"—unsophisticated hackers who follow a step-by-step script to implement an exploit developed by others. Timely use of patches blocks this sort of scripted attack.

12.2 Malicious Code

"Malware" is software whose purpose is to harm the system that loads it. Malware applications can arrive as file attachments to e-mails or as executable software that is initiated through some form of network connection. These applications can hijack the computer and make it a "zombie" machine under the control of the external party. Files can be read or stolen and additional software attacks can be launched with the coordination of the malware application.

Currently, there is a very thin line between online threats (such as spyware and adware applications, defined further in Chapter 5) and truly destructive malware. All of these will, at best, consume system resources, provide a means for outsiders to view a portion of a machine's contents and even track the activities of the machines' users.

12.3 Layered Attacks

A threat can be designed and deployed to attack an information system at any number of layers—from the network to the system to any of the applications that reside in between.

Network-layer attacks exploit the basic network protocol in order to gain any available advantage. These attacks generally involve "spoofing," or falsifying, a network address so that a computer sends data to an intruder rather than the proper recipient or destination. Other attacks can involve service disruptions through a denial of service (DoS) attack—a brute force method that overloads the capacity of a website's domain to respond to incoming requests such that it renders the server inoperable.

Applications that "listen" to Internet server ports in order to track suspicious activity often themselves contain vulnerabilities that may allow a hacker to gain access. A good preventive strategy is to deactivate unnecessary network services and block unused or idle network ports so that the scope of any vulnerability is minimized.

Firewalls, located on both network perimeters and hosts, are generally fairly effective at preventing network-layer attacks.

Application-layer attacks exploit flaws in the network applications that are installed on the network servers. Such weaknesses exist in web browsers, e-mail server software, network routing software and other standard enterprise applications. This constitutes the most common type of exploit because there are so many different possibilities for the hacker to consider.[29] A key way to prevent application attacks is to regularly apply all relevant and current patches and updates to applications. Another common practice is to disable all unnecessary services that listen for network traffic in case they contain a vulnerability that can be exploited.

12.4 Disaster Recovery

Information security threats also can originate from beyond the human or technical realms—such as from catastrophes, unforeseen events and acts of nature.

Localized emergencies such as fires can pose a significant risk for data loss. Backup tapes or other media should be stored in a location away from the organization to ensure greater protection. Key servers or other devices can be kept in an off-site data storage center designed for mission-critical systems. These centers are continuously monitored, environmentally controlled with backup systems, and contain advanced fire-suppression systems.

Natural disasters such as tornados, earthquakes and hurricanes are admittedly very difficult to prepare for. These natural emergencies can affect a geographically significant area and bring considerable destruction. If an organization is located in an area prone to these types of events, it may be advisable to consider geographical co-location. Under this arrangement, the data center is replicated in another location and contains data fail-over capacity. A challenge to co-location is keeping the data synchronized, as well as maintaining system security at more locations. Depending on the organization's business requirements, this may be a simple or extremely costly task.

When planning for catastrophic loss, an organization should consider the possibility that the physical systems (the facilities themselves and everything contained within) may be destroyed. The remedial options range from simply purchasing new hardware to maintaining a replicated data center in another location that can be turned operational if needed. Obviously, these plans involve vastly different levels of cost and complexity. The business requirements of an organization will determine the type of contingency planning, insurance and other responses to interruptions of business continuity.

While recovery of data and hardware is frequently planned for, application recovery is too often overlooked. This can become a significant problem if the organization uses custom applications. But even purchasing replacement "off the shelf" programs for installation may not be as simple as reinstalling existing software. Many programs have complex licensing procedures that may take days or longer to process if not planned for in advance.

12.5 Business Continuity Management

To plan for these external security threats or emergencies, organizations should also implement business continuity management systems well in advance in order to protect, maintain and recover critical processes and systems.

Regular data backups are an important part of any business continuance plan: They create a system record that can be an invaluable forensic tool in determining the timing, origin and nature of a data event (access, breach or loss).

While most people consider information security in terms of hackers and exploits, data can be lost just as easily through more mundane means such as lack of personnel oversight or misplaced documents and electronic files. In the event of data loss from any cause, backups are essential to maintaining business functionality. They also provide a baseline in the event of a security breach to better gauge what data may have been lost and thus requires recovery. Backups can be used to determine if any data has been altered or even aid in tracking an attacker who has erased system logs.

The data contained on backups must be protected from unauthorized access. The actual storage file backups should be maintained in a physically secure location; if the data is sensitive, it should be encrypted. Access to backups must be protected as effectively as access to the original data, and thus access to backups must be tightly controlled.[30]

A backup is only as good as its recoverability. Emergency data recovery plans should be made and tested by the organization, and backups should be evaluated regularly to verify the efficacy of data recoverability. Data recovery procedures are typically integrated with other disaster contingency and business continuity plans that an organization may have in place.

Most data is stored within databases. Therefore, proper database management is central to ensuring effective privacy. The process of determining who should have access to the information stored in these databases should take into consideration that database administrators do not need access to the information in order to manage the database. The use of "database views" is valuable in restricting access to sensitive data contained within databases.

A data security professional should work with business professionals to ensure that the core business functions will continue to operate after any emergency.

13. Incident Management and Data Breach Notification

Despite the strongest software tools, the best employee and awareness training programs, the most well developed contingency plan and the best communicated and rehearsed business continuance procedures, data breaches can—and inevitably will—occur. It simply isn't possible to prevent them completely. Thus organizations need to be prepared for incident management and data breach notification.

The life cycle of incident management can be thought of as a four-step process, as illustrated in Figure 4-2.

Figure 4-2: Life Cycle of Incident Management

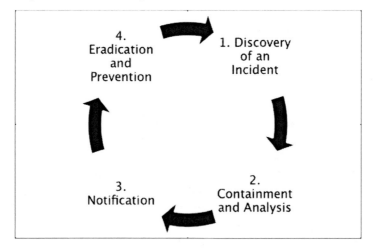

13.1 Discovery of an Incident

The methods employed by rogue employees, hackers and exploit artists are often revealed in basic behaviors that can be detected and observed by a discriminating information security professional or software. These behaviors include multiple failed system login attempts; use of long-idle or dormant access accounts; unexplained changes in access permissions; activity during nonbusiness hours; use of unauthorized new accounts, files or applications; and gaps in system logs.

The following types of situations might lead to discovering an incident:

- Numerous failed login attempts could indicate that someone is trying to access the system by guessing a password. The account should be monitored for further activity if not deactivated promptly.

- The sudden use of an idle or long-dormant access account may indicate the compromise of a system. A dormant account may be an account that was created or modified by an intruder for later use. Usage should be monitored and dormant accounts deleted or verified as to why they are not in use.

- Use of computer systems during off-hours, when the office is normally closed, is another clue. Atypical computer usage may indicate that a rogue employee is using the network for personal gain, such as downloading of confidential and proprietary information. Hackers also often try to break into a system during nonwork hours in hopes that they will not be detected until the next business day.

- The presence of an unauthorized access account (a new account not created by the system administrator) is itself strong evidence of a security compromise. Since only a "super-user" (system administrator) holds the authority to create an access account, the existence of an unauthorized account requires the presumption that such super-user privileges have been compromised and ought to be re-architected entirely.

- The presence of unfamiliar programs or files is another indication of a breach. Hackers often leave programs or files behind during their virtual "travels" for the purpose of collecting data or permitting return access. However, the only real way to know that a file does not belong to a specific directory is to know what files *do* belong. This requires a full system audit with complete documentation that identifies all authorized files by name, variety and size. Programs are available that can automate this laborious process.[31]

- Weak user passwords or psychological manipulation (pretexting or social engineering) may be used to gain low-level access to a system. The hacker will then elevate the privileges of that account to gain more access. Unexplained elevation of privileges is a sure sign of a system compromise.

- Changes in file permissions can be a significant clue to unauthorized access. Only users with privileges equal to that of the file have the ability to make any such changes. Therefore, unauthorized changes to the permissions of a super-user file indicate a compromise of the super-user account.

- The presence of unknown devices connecting to the network may indicate removable media that employees are using to download and extract personally identifiable information. These removable media, such as USB sticks, can be lost or stolen.

- Gaps in system logs are possibly the most common way of discovering a system compromise. In an attempt to hide his/her tracks, a hacker will attempt to delete those logs that automatically record exploits. Since log files are generally very long transcripts of all system activities, it can be difficult to detect any discernible gaps. Scripts and programs can automate the task of log validation.

- Alerts or red flags from data loss prevention software may indicate that employees are attempting to send e-mails containing protected information outside the organization. Misuse of the e-mail system may be inadvertent due to a lack of training or understanding of proper e-mail protocol, or may be intentional.

- Inventories of laptops, mobile devices or backup tapes do not match up with the number of devices currently in circulation or in storage. Mismatches against an inventory may be an indication that hardware or devices have been lost or stolen.

It is considered good practice to establish a highly secure log host. This provides a secure location for logs to reside and a single point for monitoring logs from all the systems on a network.[32] Additionally, system logs can be simultaneously written on the local system and on a remote system and then periodically compared. If the second log can be written to write-once media like a CD-ROM or a printer, then you can know for sure that the second source is valid.

It is important to keep in mind that while system failures and malicious attacks are typical causes of data breaches, two of the most common sources of data breaches are third-party mistakes and employee negligence. For example, in the healthcare industry in 2011, 49 percent of organizations experienced data incidents caused by a lost or stolen computing device, 46 percent experienced a data breach due to a third-party error, and 41 percent experienced a breach caused by an unintentional employee action.[33] Therefore, security personnel must stress to employees the importance of reporting errors, as they are likely the main method of detecting non-IT-related breaches. Contractual obligations requiring third-party vendors to notify the organization of any incident that involves the organization's data are also an important means of discovering incidents. Without such reporting obligations, many errors, such as lost paper records or break-ins to the premises of third-party partners, may occur without the organization's knowledge.

13.2 Containment and Analysis

Once discovered, the next step is containment and analysis. Immediate response to incidents is especially important if that compromise causes a systemwide failure, leads to a breach that triggers legal notification obligations or poses a risk of harm to individuals.

Containment involves stopping the unauthorized practice, recovering the records, shutting down the system that was breached, revoking access or correcting any weakness in physical security. It may also involve notifying the police if criminal activity or theft was involved. In cases of e-mail errors, certain services may offer recall functions that can delete any e-mails sent before they are read. To contain data breaches where a laptop or smartphone is lost, some devices have remote wipe technology.

Some initial analysis will need to be performed to determine which systems and networks were impacted. It is a priority to limit use of a network or system that has been compromised until forensic experts can analyze the system fully and verify its condition. Most people do not know that even logging into a system can destroy important evidence. If a system has been compromised, it should be immediately disconnected from the network and powered down (depending on the computer operating system and whether the shutdown would lose any valuable data), the hard drive should be removed, and data restored from backup onto a new drive. It is important that a full system audit be performed to make sure that the vulnerability that was once exploited is not inadvertently restored or reactivated.

After initial containment, an in-depth, complete analysis and documentation of the incident is required. In IT-related incidents, computer forensics can offer the necessary details to troubleshoot a security breach. These details can be used in negotiations with other affected parties or in litigation that may result.

> **Computer forensics** *is the discipline of assessing and examining an information system for relevant clues after it has been compromised by an exploit.*

Assessing forensic information after a network intrusion requires a trained professional. Even the most novice hacker will take steps to cover tracks, making it difficult to collect any relevant evidence along the network path. A computer forensic expert should be consulted in constructing a policy or procedure so as to ensure that the integrity and lasting value of the forensics process are assured.

The admissibility of computer forensic evidence in legal proceedings can be quite complex. For evidence to be admissible, it must be proven that the information presented has not been changed or altered. However, computers are constantly writing and rewriting data, and a significant amount of forensic evidence can be altered or even lost entirely just by logging in to a compromised system.

The aim of forensics is to prevent further damage resulting from the incident, thus limiting the potential liabilities and minimizing potential damage. The results should indicate how the system was exploited and what was compromised, which can help IT formulate a plan for remedying the exploit.

Where a data breach was caused by inadvertent employee error or accidental loss of storage media, computer forensics can also help determine the scope of any data that may have been impacted by the error or data loss.

For incidents involving paper records or third parties, containment may be more difficult. It may be hard to recover paper documents that have been lost. Other than conducting a search for the paper records, and trying to establish their path, it may be impossible to contain the breach.

When an incident takes place at a third-party partner's site, there may be resistance to the organization's efforts to perform analysis or investigation of the third party's systems and employees. Contractual arrangements need to be in place, delineating each party's obligations in response to a breach, including containment, investigation and analysis.

The analysis of an incident will need to determine what type of information was affected (e.g., personally identifiable information, intellectual property, trade secrets, etc.), the number of people who were impacted, and the groups that were impacted (employees, customers, out-of-state residents). This analysis will inform the organization's notification obligations.

13.3 Notification

Beginning with Senate Bill 1386 in California in 2003, notification following a data breach became a legal requirement. This requirement spread throughout the United States (at the time of writing, 46 states and the District of Columbia have breach notification laws) and to many parts of the world, including Germany, Austria, South Korea, and Mexico. At the time of writing, Canada, the United States, France, the Philippines, and many other jurisdictions around the world are all considering federal and/or state or provincial laws. Also, a European Union–wide notification requirement is being considered.[34] Even if not legally required, many organizations and regulators view notification as a mandatory practice.

Data Breach

A data breach is an incident where personally identifiable information has been lost or subject to unauthorized acquisition, access, disclosure or destruction in a manner that compromises its security, confidentiality or integrity.

Factors that vary based on the laws include:

- The trigger for notification
- Whom to notify
- Timing of notification
- Contents of notices
- Methods of providing notification

13.3.1 Trigger for Notification

In some jurisdictions, organizations are legally required to notify affected individuals only if there is some degree of harm to the individual, while in other jurisdictions all data breaches must be notified. Types of harm that may result from a breach include risks to personal safety, identity theft, financial loss, loss of business or employment opportunities, and humiliation or embarrassment.

Notification may be limited to circumstances where the harm is serious or significant. The level of risk posed by harm depends on factors such as the type and amount of personal information involved, extent and cause of the breach (i.e., was it malicious or inadvertent), who was affected by the breach and any foreseeable harm. Even if not legally obliged to provide notification, an organization may wish to notify affected individuals as a best practice where there is a high degree of risk to them and they may be able to take steps to protect themselves.

In many cases, personal information that is protected by means like encryption, such that it cannot be read, need not be notified due to the remote possibility of harm.

13.3.2 Whom to Notify

Whom to notify is a key issue that must be determined. Possible recipients of a breach report include:

- Regulators
- Law enforcement
- Affected individuals
- Insurers
- Any relevant service providers (e.g., call center support or insurance providers)
- The media
- Any other stakeholders (e.g., shareholders or employees)

13.3.3 When to Notify

The desire for expedient notification to allow individuals to mitigate any risk of harm may need to be balanced against legal requirements and the need to fully understand the scope of the breach to avoid overnotification (e.g., where fewer individuals were affected than originally believed). The timing of notification varies by law and may range from 24 hours to "in the most expedient time possible" to "within a reasonable amount of time." Some laws provide that organizations may delay notification when law enforcement is investigating the breach, or when the delay is necessary to restore the reasonable integrity of the information systems.

13.3.4 What to Include in Notification

The content of notifications will vary depending on who is being notified. Regulators may want greater information about the cause and scope of the breach, while it may be more important for individuals to learn about steps they can take to protect themselves from fallout.

What should be included in the notification may be dictated by law, but may include:

- The nature of the incident in general terms
- Type of personal information breached
- Any assistance the organization is offering the individual (e.g., credit monitoring, replacing credit or debit cards, identity theft insurance, etc.)
- Any steps the individual can take to protect himself
- A point of contact within the organization from whom the individual can seek more information about the breach

13.3.5 How to Notify

Depending on the availability of contact information and the number of affected individuals, methods of notification may include direct mail, telephone, e-mail, facsimile and publication of a notice in a general-circulation newspaper or on the organization's website. Although not currently addressed under the laws, some organizations consider alternative methods of notification, such as through social networking sites or via text messages, where these are the ordinary methods used to communicate with the affected individuals. The general rule is that the organization in the direct relationship with the individual is the one that provides notification. Thus, if a breach occurs at an organization's service provider, the organization notifies individuals, but the service provider should be under contractual obligation to notify the organization.

13.4 Eradication and Prevention

The final step of incident management is investigating the root cause of the breach, with a view to taking steps to remediate any gaps discovered in security, processes or training. A breach should be examined to determine if there are systemic problems that need to be addressed or whether it was an isolated incident. Maintaining an internal report of all breaches allows the organization to monitor for patterns that would underlie systemic issues.

When regulators have been involved in the aftermath of a breach, they have demanded that organizations take certain steps to prevent breaches in the future. For example, these might include:

- Implementing a comprehensive information security program reasonably designed to protect the security, confidentiality and integrity of personal information.[35] Program elements may include appointing staff to be accountable for the program, conducting risk assessments and implementing employee training.

- Implementing administrative, technical and physical safeguards that are proportionate to the organization's size and complexity, nature and scope of the organization's activities and sensitivity of the personal information held.[36]

- Implementing encryption or using higher encryption standards.[37]

- Updating privacy notices and retention schedules.[38]

- Implementing additional security measures, such as monitoring software, adding firewalls and changing passwords.[39]

Complete documentation of incidents should be maintained to share with any regulators, as well as to defend against class action lawsuits that may arise as a result of the data breach. Documentation may include details on the cause and scope of the incident, date the incident was discovered and how it was discovered, who was notified and what they were notified of, and the steps the organization has taken to mitigate any harm.

Given that employee negligence or error is one of the leading causes of data breaches, employees need to be trained on how to protect data and what to do in the event of a breach. The organization must instill a culture of privacy, having every employee recognize his or her role in achieving a secure environment. Training should include basic awareness training for frontline employees and more detailed privacy instruction for those with access to personally identifiable information. Refresher training can take place following a breach event, using real-world examples of what has occurred either within the organization or at other similarly situated organizations. Continual privacy education and verbal and written reminders can help keep privacy in the forefront of employees' minds. Any time the incident response protocol is changed, employees should be provided an update. The organizational culture must also foster an atmosphere where employees feel protected if they report a suspected or actual data breach; employees will underreport if they feel their job is in jeopardy due to their mistake.

As the end of the incident life cycle is reached, the organization should be better positioned to discover and respond to any subsequent events and proceed through the life cycle with greater familiarity in the future. A detailed incident response plan should be developed that specifies how the enterprise will address an incident the moment it has been detected. This plan should include staff reporting obligations to escalate any instances of actual or possible incidents to management, the privacy office or any other designated official.

14. Monitoring and Compliance

Administrative controls are policies that organizations can use to demonstrate that they handle data responsibly and comply with relevant laws and regulations. This can be challenging in a global setting because these requirements vary widely. Thus, it is important to build a system of auditing and monitoring into your security program early, along with administrative, technical and physical controls.

14.1 Self-Assessments and Third-Party Audits

As a best practice, an organization should complete a self-assessment of its data storage and processing methods on a regular basis. Particular attention should be paid to whether information privacy and security procedures are fully compliant—to published policy as well as to applicable laws and regulations. These assessments may be conducted by privacy staff, a compliance department or an internal audit department. Assessment results should be analyzed and action plans developed to remediate any policy deficiencies with the affected line of business. The results of assessments should also be analyzed in light of any new changes in regulations and laws, and policy or practices adjusted accordingly. The assessment should also take into account changing business strategies or expectations of the company from customers and clients.

Some organizations may prefer or require that a complete assessment be conducted by an authorized third-party auditor. A privacy policy audit conducted by a third party is an effective means of assessing compliance with the policy and locating areas that need better security measures. An audit may also provide information useful for streamlining the data sharing or transfer processes. Large companies in particular may find a third-party audit useful in reviewing what may be a very complicated policy and data management infrastructure. Third-party auditors can leverage additional experience or expertise from the industry in which the audited organization operates—and share industry standards and best practices that may serve to benefit the audited organization.

15. Summary

Information security is a central business function precisely because information technology enables virtually every other type of business activity within the organization. Security ensures a high level of confidence in information management and must itself be considered a formal business function for the organization to be successful. Security-enabling technologies, policies and methods are integral parts of any successful privacy program and must be included in an organization's business life cycle from design through implementation to retirement.

Effective information security can become a significant financial investment for an organization. It is important for privacy and information security professionals to work closely to explain to executive management (and other stakeholders in the organization) the importance of effective information security measures. Privacy and information security measures together serve as the bedrock of the consumer and stakeholder trust the organization establishes and must continue to build over time.

Endnotes

1   Various tools are available to assist in mapping out systems on your network. These can be helpful because they give you the same perspective on the network as someone trying to infiltrate it. Be careful in downloading software from these sites as it is a common practice to code backdoor exploits into the software. Some of these tools are available at www.treachery.net/tools. A tool popular with both network and security administrators and hackers is n-map, a network-mapping tool available at www.insecure.org (note: the tool is available for Windows, but is much more robust for Linux).

2   A fairly comprehensive database of whitepapers on auditing best practices is available at www.sans.org/reading_room/whitepapers/auditing/.

3   For more information on system logs, see Seham Mohamed GadAllah, "The Importance of Logging and Traffic Monitoring for Information Security," Dec. 2003, www.sans.org/reading_room/whitepapers/logging/importance-logging-traffic-monitoring-information-security_1379.

4   GAO, "Technology Assessment: Cybersecurity for Critical Infrastructure Protection," May 2004, 151, www.gao.gov/new.items/d04321.pdf.

5   Id. at 24.

6   GAO, "Information Security: Weak Controls Place Interior's Financial and Other Data at Risk," July 3, 2001, 14, www.gao.gov/new.items/d01615.pdf.

7   Id.

8   See Keith MacLeod, "Patch Management and the Need for Metrics," July 2004, www.sans.org/rr/whitepapers/bestprac/1461.php.

9   For more information on the importance of physical security, see Bob Pagoria, "Implementing Robust Physical Security," July 13, 2004, www.sans.org/reading_room/whitepapers/physcial/implementing-robust-physical-security_1447.

10 For more information on the security threat posed by iPods, see Simon Dawson, "Information Theft," *Legalweek*, June 9, 2005.

11 Some are beginning to explore the risks to data security posed by camera phones and Bluetooth phones. See Russell Robinson, "Surviving the Camera Phone Phenomenon: An Analysis of Personal & Corporate Security," Feb. 2004, www.sans.org/rr/whitepapers/privacy/1387.php.

12 See Daniel Oxenhandler, "Designing a Secure Local Area Network," 2003, www.sans.org/rr/whitepapers/bestprac/853.php.

13 For one example of how to mitigate extranet risks, see "Business Partner VPN: Needed Now," 2003, www.sans.org/rr/whitepapers/vpns/880.php.

14 See Michael Stines, "Remote Access VPN—Security Concerns and Policy Enforcement," 2003, www.sans.org/reading_room/whitepapers/vpns/remote-access-vpn-security-concerns-policy-enforcement_881.

15 For more information about digital signatures, see Walter Goulet, "Analyzing Enterprise PKI Deployments," August 4, 2009, www.sans.org/reading_room/whitepapers/auditing/analyzing-enterprise-pki-deployments_33284.

16 *Id.*

17 For more information on the types of threats internal users pose and ways of mitigating those risks, see Charles Rhodes, "The Internal Threat to Security or Users Can Really Mess Things Up," 2003, www.sans.org/rr/whitepapers/bestprac/856.php.

18 This follows the principle of least privilege, a concept popularized by the NSA. For information on implementing this principle, see Jeff Langford, "Implementing Least Privilege at your Enterprise," July 5, 2003, www.sans.org/rr/whitepapers/bestprac/1188.php.

19 For more information on the importance of incorporating end users into data security models and the threats posed to end-user systems, see Andrew Conry-Murray, "Securing End Users from Attack," *Network Magazine*, Oct. 5, 2002.

20 Paul Festa and Lisa Bowman, "Computers Hinder Paper Shredders," Feb. 4, 2002, www.news.cnet.com/2100-1023-829004.html.

21 Justin Pope, "Haunted by Ghosts of Hard Drives Past," Jan. 16, 2003, www.cbsnews.com/stories/2003/01/16/tech/main536774.shtml.

22 For an example of how one company maintained security over outsourced IT, see Leslie Martinez, "Retain Control of Security (Even in the Wake of an IT Outsource)," Feb. 2003, www.sans.org/reading_room/whitepapers/casestudies/retain-control-security-even-wake-outsource_1244.

23 Christopher Koch, "Don't Maroon Security," *CIO Magazine*, May 15, 2005.

24 For a more complete introduction to PKI, see ArticSoft, "Introduction to Public Key Infrastructure," Feb. 2, 2003, www.articsoft.com/public_key_infrastructure.htm.

25 For more detailed information on PKI, see Duncan Wood, "PKI, the What, the Why, and the How," 2002, www.sans.org/reading_room/whitepapers/vpns/pki-what-why_764.

26 For information on public key encryption generally, and one of its most popular implementations, PGP (Pretty Good Privacy), see "How PGP Works," 1999, www.pgpi.org/doc/pgpintro.

27 For more information on vectoring or perimeter-based virus protection, see Daniel Boyd, "Scanning for Viruses," Feb. 2003, www.sans.org/reading_room/whitepapers/firewalls/scanning-viruses_995.

28 *Guide to Computer Security Log Management*, National Institute of Standards and Technology Special Publication 800-92, http://csrc.nist.gov/publications/nistpubs/800-92/SP800-92.pdf.

29 Justin Crist, "Web Based Attacks," 2007, www.sans.org/reading_room/whitepapers/application/web-based-attacks_2053).

30 For more information on securing centralized data backups, see Scott M. Parrish, "Security Considerations for Enterprise Level Backups," 2002, www.sans.org/reading_room/whitepapers/backup/security-considerations-enterprise-level-backups_515.

31 Tripwire is a perennial favorite for this task. The program is available in open source format from http://sourceforge.net/projects/tripwire/or together with commercial services and add-on features from companies like Tripwire Inc. at www.tripwire.com.

32 See Nathaniel Hall, "Creating a Secure Linux Logging System," Oct. 2004, www.sans.org/reading_room/whitepapers/logging/creating-secure-linux-logging-system_1529; Gregory Lalla, "Centralizing Event Logs on Windows 2000," Feb. 2003, www.sans.org/reading_room/whitepapers/logging/centralizing-event-logs-windows-2000_902; or David Swift, "Successful SIEM and Log Management Strategies for Audit and Compliance," 2010, www.sans.org/reading_room/whitepapers/auditing/successful-siem-log-management-strategies-audit-compliance_33528.

33 Ponemon Institute, Second Annual Benchmark Study on Patient Privacy and Data Security, Dec. 2011. These numbers reach a total greater than 100% because the same organization may have experienced several data breach incidents caused by different events over the course of one year.

34 In Article 4 of Directive 2002/58/EC, the EU implemented a requirement for providers of publicly available electronic communications services to inform subscribers concerning risks of breaches to its network security. The EU is currently revising its data protection framework, and among the changes would be a breach notification obligation on any data controller that experiences a personal data breach that would likely adversely affect the protection of personal data or privacy of the data subject.

35 *In re* the *TJX Companies, Inc.* FTC File No. 072-3055, Agreement Containing Consent Order; *in re Twitter, Inc.*, FTC File No. 0923093. Agreement Containing Consent Order.

36 *Id.*

37 Encryption of mobile devices has become a common element of Data Protection Act 1998, Undertakings Entered into with the Information Commissioner's Office in the United Kingdom. For examples, see the Undertaking with Richard Dominic Preston, following the theft of an unencrypted laptop, www.ico.gov.uk/what_we_cover/taking_action/~/media/documents/library/Data_Protection/Notices/richard_dominic_preston_preston_revised_undertaking.ashx, or the Undertaking with Godalming College, following the transmission of unencrypted e-mail containing personal data, www.ico.gov.uk/what_we_cover/taking_action/~/media/documents/library/Data_Protection/Notices/godalming_college_undertaking.ashx.

38 Report of an Investigation into the Security, Collection, and Retention of Personal Information: TJX Companies Inc./Winners Merchant International L.P., Office of the Privacy Commissioner of Canada and the Office of the Information and Privacy Commissioner of Alberta.

39 Own Motion Investigation of Sony PlayStation Network/Qriocity by the Office of the Australian Information Commissioner. The commissioner did not order the Sony PlayStation Network to implement these changes following a breach of its network; however, the commissioner found that these additional security measures implemented following the breach helped demonstrate that Sony had taken reasonable steps to ensure the security of its customers' personal data.

CHAPTER FIVE

Online Privacy

Using Personal Information on Websites
and Other Internet Technologies

1. Overview of Web Technologies

The Internet is a global system of interconnected networks that links millions of computers around the world and can be accessed by computers and other electronic devices anywhere, instantaneously.

The precursor to the Internet we know today was the ARPAnet, a military computer network developed in the early 1960s by the U.S. Advance Research Projects Agency (ARPA). The ARPAnet established a secure means for the exchange of military information and expanded to scientific research when the National Science Foundation became involved with the network in the early 1970s.[1]

Far in time and size from its origins, the Internet today has the same basic architecture as when it was first designed. Data on the vast network is transferred by shuttling small pieces of information known as data "packets" from one computer to the next. Data is disassembled into packets on transmission, scattered throughout the network while in transit and then dynamically reassembled upon arrival at the destination computer. This open and dynamic nature of the Internet enables its speed, functionality and continued growth but—as will be described later in this chapter—also exposes it to certain information privacy vulnerabilities.

1.1 The World Wide Web

The World Wide Web is an information-sharing model that is built on top of the Internet. It was first designed to facilitate the exchange not just of text-based information—as the Internet primarily did originally—but also graphic images, interactive document files and other "richer" information formats.

The web historically functioned based on two key technologies:

1. **Hypertext transfer protocol (HTTP)**, an application protocol that manages data communications over the Internet. HTTP defines how messages are formatted and transmitted over a TCP/IP network (defined below) for websites. Further, it defines what actions web servers and web browsers take in response to various commands.

2. **Hypertext markup language (HTML)**, a content-authoring language used to create web pages. The web browser interprets the HTML markup language within a web page to determine how the content on the page should be rendered. Document "tags" can be used to format and lay out a web page's content and to "hyperlink"—connect dynamically—to other web content. Forms, links, pictures and text may all be added with minimal commands. Headings are also embedded into the text and are used by web servers to process commands and return data with each request.[2]

Sir Tim Berners-Lee, a British physicist working out of the Switzerland-based particle physics laboratory known as CERN, developed the HTML authoring language in the early 1990s. Berners-Lee recognized the inherent limitations of the early Internet and advanced the HTML language as a means for research scientists such as himself to dynamically tie documents and files together—a capability he referred to as "hyperlinking."

Also at that time, the U.S.-based National Center for Supercomputing Applications (NCSA) developed the first web browser application, Mozilla. This browser software offered, for the first time, a user-friendly interface through which the ever-evolving web documents and websites could be viewed from a personal computer. Mark Andreessen, an NCSA student and young author of Mozilla, went on to form Netscape Communications and create the browser that became known as Netscape, a derivative of the earlier Mozilla.

HTML has continuously evolved since it was first developed in the 1990s. Today, many browsers support features of HTML5, the fifth and most recent version of the HTML standard. HTML5 has new capabilities and features, such as the ability to run video, audio and animation directly from websites without the need for a plug-in, a piece of software that runs in the browser and renders media such as audio or video. Though still in draft form as of 2012 (with a target release date of 2014 for the HTML5 standard), HTML5 has significant implications for the rapidly expanding mobile ecosystem, as many mobile devices do not support Flash (discussed further below).[3] Another feature of HTML5 is the ability to store information offline, in web applications that can run when not connected to the Internet.

Extensible markup language (XML) is another language that facilitates the transport, creation, retrieval and storage of documents. Similar to HTML, XML uses tags to describe the contents of a web page or file. HTML describes the content of a web page in terms of how it should be displayed. Unlike HTML, XML describes content of a web page in terms of the data that is being produced, potentially creating automatic processing of data in ways that may require attention for privacy issues.[4]

The web browser software is considered a "web client" application in that it is used to navigate the web and retrieve web content from web servers for viewing. Some web server firewalls also function as a web client.[5] To protect the inner system, the firewall will interact with the inner web proxy as a client, and then relay the same request out to the web server. By forcing a two-step process, the inner system never has a direct network connection to the external web.

Two of the more common web browser–level functions are URLs and hyperlinks.

- A **URL (uniform resource locator)** is the address of documents and other content that are located on a web server; specifically, the letter and number coordinates that an end user submits to the web browser to instruct it to connect with the desired web server (website). An example of a URL is "http://www.privacyassociation.org." This URL contains an HTTP prefix to indicate its use of the protocol, www to signify a location on the World Wide Web, a domain name (e.g., the web server name) and an indicator of the top-level domain (e.g., "com" for a commercial organization, "org" for an organization, "gov" for government, "edu" for an educational institution, or a two-letter country code, such as UK for United Kingdom or JP for Japan).[6]

- A **hyperlink** is used to connect an end user to other websites, parts of websites and/or web-enabled services. The URL of another site is embedded in the HTML code of a site, so that when certain words or images are selected through the web browser, the end user is transported to the destination website or page.

1.2 Web Infrastructure

The web is built upon a conglomeration of hardware and software technologies that include server computers, client applications (such as browsers, discussed above) and various networking protocols.

- A **web server** is a computer that is connected to the Internet, hosts web content and is configured to share that content. Documents that are viewed on the web are actually located on individual web servers and accessed by a browser.

- A **proxy server** is an intermediary server that provides a gateway to the web. Employee access to the web often goes through a proxy server. A proxy server typically masks what is happening behind the organization's firewall, so that an outside website sees only the IP address and other characteristics of the proxy server, and not detailed information about which part of an organization is communicating with the outside website. A proxy server generally logs each user interaction, filters out malicious software downloads, and improves performance by caching popular, regularly-fetched content.

- **Caching** occurs when web browsers and proxy servers save a local copy of the downloaded content, reducing the need to download the same content again. To protect privacy, pages that display personal information should be set to prohibit caching.

- A **web server log** is sometimes automatically created when a visitor requests a web page. Examples of the information automatically logged include the IP address of the visitor, the date and time of the web page request, the URL of the requested filed, the URL of the visitor immediately prior to the web page request, and the visitor's web browser type and computer operating system. Depending on how the web server is configured, it is possible for personal information such as usernames to appear in web server logs. As discussed in Chapter 1, IP addresses themselves, and thus web server logs containing them, are considered personal information by some regulators but not others.

The following additional terms are essential in understanding the online privacy concepts to be addressed in this chapter.

- The **Internet protocol (IP)** specifies the format of data packets that travel over the Internet and also provides the appropriate addressing protocol. An IP address is a unique number assigned to each connected device—it is similar to a phone number because the IP address shows where data should be sent from the website. An Internet service provider often assigns a new IP address on a session-by-session basis. When the IP address used by an individual thus shifts with each session, this approach is referred to as a "dynamic" IP address. Conversely, "static" IP addresses have become more common in recent years; a static IP address remains the same over time. In such cases, a website can use the static IP address as a way to recognize a device that returns to the site.[7] This persistent link to a device is the basis in some countries for considering an IP address as personal information, because of the greater likelihood that data can be linked to a specific user.[8] As mentioned in Chapter 1, the next generation of the Internet protocol, IPv6, has additional privacy concerns because the address of the computing device is by default based on hardware characteristics of the device's networking interface, allowing for easier tracking of computing devices as they move between networks.

- **Transmission-control protocol (TCP)** enables two devices to establish a stream-oriented reliable data connection. A combination of TCP and IP is used to send data over the Internet. Data is sent in the form of packets, which contain message content and a heading that specifies the destination of the packet.

- The **secure sockets layer (SSL)** is the protocol for establishing a secure connection for transmission and facilitates much of the online commerce (shopping and purchasing) that occurs on the Internet today. For example, HTTPS, a secure form of HTTP, is an SSL application used in password exchanges or e-commerce. Its Netscape creators state, "The primary goal of the SSL Protocol is to provide privacy and reliability between two communicating applications."[9] There are three properties to the protocol: (1) The connection is private; (2) the peer's identity can be authenticated using asymmetric, or public key, cryptography; and (3) the connection is reliable.[10]

- **Transport layer security (TLS)** is a protocol that ensures privacy between client-server applications and Internet users of the applications. When a server and client communicate, TLS secures the connection to ensure that no third party can eavesdrop on or corrupt the message. TLS is a successor to SSL.

- **Javascript** is a scripting language used to produce a more interactive and dynamic website. However, the language should be used with the recognition that some browsers still do not support it.[11] Javascript has vulnerabilities and problems interacting with some programs and systems.[12] A common malicious practice is cross-site scripting, which is discussed later in this chapter. Simple additions, like an infinite loop, can overwhelm the memory and impose a denial of service attack. Generally, to prevent such attacks, one should be aware of the entity from which one is downloading a program.

- **Flash** is a bandwidth-friendly interactive animation and video technology that has been widely used to enliven web pages and advertisements. Compatibility and security problems, however, have led to a decrease in use. Some security experts now discourage users from installing Flash.[13] As HTML5 becomes more widely adopted and as the mobile computing environment grows, use of external plug-ins such as Flash may diminish; in November 2011, Adobe told developers that it no longer plans to develop future versions of its Flash Player for mobile browsers.[14]

2. Privacy Considerations for Online Information

When individuals provide information about themselves through the Internet—whether through a social networking site, online shopping transaction, or otherwise— they reasonably expect this information to be protected. However, the global nature of the networked technologies today inherently places this information at risk of unauthorized access and use. It is critical that organizations familiarize themselves with common threats to online privacy, in order to identify and mitigate these risks.

2.1 Threats to Online Privacy

Some threats to online privacy come from **unauthorized access** to a website or other computer system. This access may be criminal behavior, such as seeking to profit in the underground economy through fraudulent use of identity credentials and related financial information. **Malware** is a term for software that is designed for malicious purposes, such as gaining the attacker unauthorized control over a remote computer. **Phishing** is a term for e-mails or other communications that are designed to trick a user into believing that he or she should provide a password, account number, or other information. The user then typically provides that information to a website controlled by the attacker. **Spear phishing** is a phishing attack that is tailored to the individual user, such as when an e-mail appears to be from the user's boss, instructing the user to provide information.

    Social engineering is a general term for how attackers can try to persuade a user to provide information or create some other sort of security vulnerability. The "social engineer" is intent on gaining access to private information and targets an individual or group within an organization that may have such access. Techniques include using an assumed identity in communications, eavesdropping on private conversations or calls, or impersonating an employee or hired worker. Social engineering contrasts with a wide array of technically based attacks, such as SQL injection, cookie poisoning or use of malware. One technical but common threat to online privacy is cross-site scripting (XSS). XSS is code injected by malicious web users into web pages viewed by other users. Often, the unauthorized content resulting from XSS appears on a web page and looks official, so the users are tricked into thinking the site is legitimate and uncorrupted. XSS is the basis for many convincing phishing attacks and browser exploits.

Other threats to online privacy can come in the ordinary course of an organization's use of personal information. For instance, a website may collect more information about visitors' behavior than is permitted by law, or may misuse information within the organization, in violation of the organization's privacy policies. As technology has evolved, there have been ongoing public debates about the extent of information that is lawful and appropriate to collect when users visit websites.

2.2 Online Privacy Notices and Methods for Communication

Online privacy notices play an important role in consumer privacy. An effective online privacy notice provides consumers with easy-to-follow guidance about how their information is being accessed, used, and protected. Notices vary in form and length, and are often used together with other indices of certified privacy protection. Notices are also often treated as enforceable promises by a company, so they should be drafted carefully.

2.2.1 Web Privacy Notices

A comprehensive privacy statement is the standard mechanism for organizations to articulate their various information practices and communicate them to the public. Such a statement is commonly—though not exclusively—made available on the organization's website. This statement covers:

- Effective date
- Scope of notice
- Types of personal information collected (both actively and passively)
- Information uses and disclosures
- Choices available to the end user
- Methods for accessing, correcting or modifying personal information or preferences
- Methods for contacting the organization or registering a dispute
- Processes for how any policy changes will be communicated to the public

The online trust verification service TRUSTe recommends the following practices when developing a basic website privacy statement:

- Say what you do; do what you say.
- Tailor disclosures to your business operations model.
- Do not treat privacy statements as disclaimers.
- Revisit your privacy statement frequently to ensure it reflects your current business and data collection practices.
- Communicate your privacy practices to your entire company.[15]

> **Trustmarks**
>
> *Trustmarks are images or logos that are displayed on websites to indicate that a business is a member of a professional organization or to show that it has passed security and privacy tests. They are designed to give customers confidence that they can safely engage in e-commerce transactions. TRUSTe, VeriSign and the Better Business Bureau are examples of trustmarks.*

Consumers have the right to know if their information can be shared with another company or used for a purpose beyond the scope of their relationship with the primary organization. This principle applies to information gathering that is conducted online. If consumers are aware that the information will be adequately safeguarded, then they can make informed decisions about allowing the secondary use of their information.[16] Limiting secondary use of personal information—unless consent is obtained—is one of the fair information practices. As discussed in Chapter 1, these practices are embodied in many national laws, such as the Privacy Act in the United States and the national laws implementing the EU Data Protection Directive, and also in international agreements such as the Organisation for Economic Co-operation and Development (OECD) Guidelines.[17]

2.2.2 Layered Notices

As data practices online have evolved and become more complex, many privacy notices have become quite lengthy. Privacy notices have often been criticized for being written in "legalese"—dense prose that is difficult to understand, written by lawyers to reduce the risk of enforcement actions. In addition, there is clear evidence that users rarely read these lengthy privacy notices.

- **Layered notices** are a response to problems with a single long notice. The basic idea is to offer "layers" that provide the key points on top in a short notice, but give users the option to read a detailed notice or click through to greater detail on particular parts of the notice.

- The **short notice** is the top layer (see the example in Figure 5-1). Often using a standard format, it summarizes the notice scope as well as basic points on the organization's practices for personal information collection, choice, use and disclosure. Details for contacting the organization on information privacy matters are also included along with links to the full notice.

- The **full notice** is the bottom layer. Often referenced from the short notice via a hyperlink, it is a comprehensive information disclosure that articulates the organization's privacy notice in its entirety. The full notice is thus available for those end users who are interested. The full notice also guides an organization's employees on permitted data practices, and can be used for accountability by enforcement agencies or the general public.

Figure 5-1: Short Privacy Notice

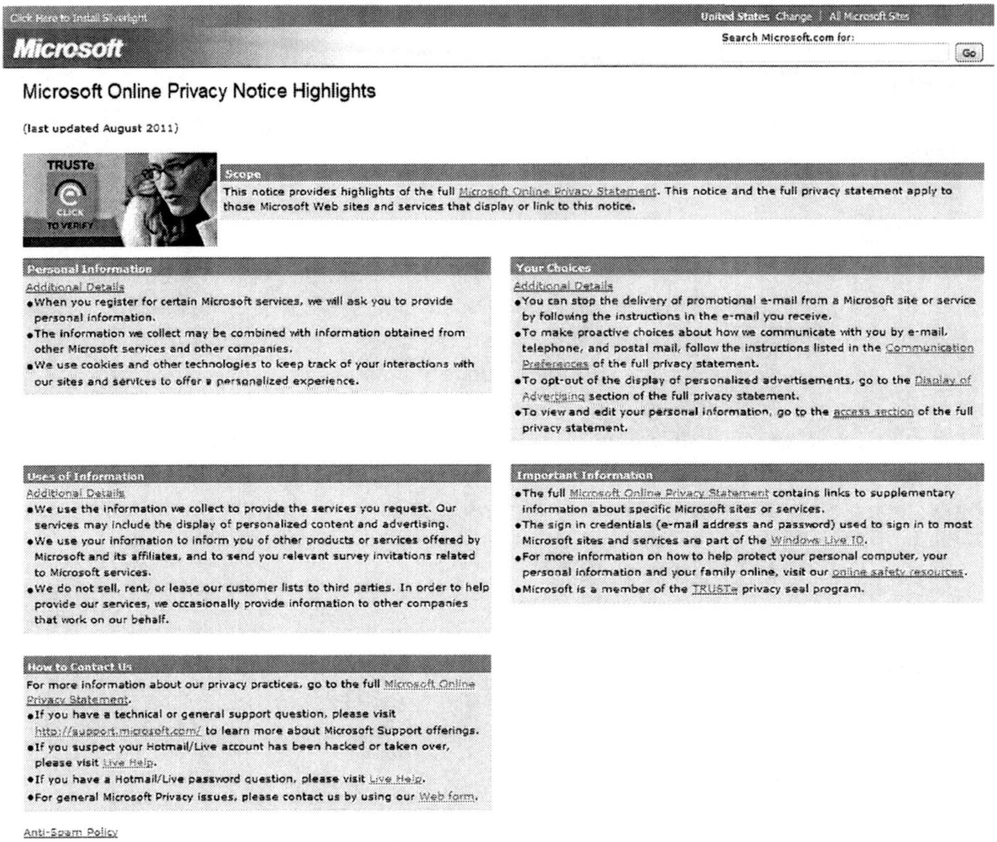

Used with permission from Microsoft.

By using "just in time" notice, which follows the principle of notice "at or before the point of information collection" or before a user accepts a service or product, organizations help facilitate meaningful choice. Many websites choose to provide a link on every page to cover passive information collection. The best choice is an easy-to-find location, in a font that is no less prominent than other links on the page.

2.3 Customer Access to Information

The same principles around information security articulated in Chapter 4 ("Information Security") also extend to the web information environment. Awareness of who has access to web-based information, when they can access it and for what reasons are all important considerations in constructing a defensible online disclosure scheme. As will be discussed further in this section, a web privacy notice should lay out what sort of notice a customer will receive, and when and how they can access their records.

The methods for providing access should be done while keeping in mind the possibility that the access request may be made by an unauthorized person, such as to carry out identity fraud. Methods for triggering access could include requiring the same information as the account (account name and password), requiring additional information about activity, requiring either option and sending the information to the account, and requiring either option and sending a one-time access code to the account.[18]

There has been some global variation in defining the scope of individuals' right to access information about themselves. Data protection and privacy professionals thus should consider which laws and policies apply to an individual's request for access.

The EU Data Protection Directive emphasizes the data subject's fundamental right to access and correct personal information about the data subject. Article 10 affirmatively states the rights of data subjects to have access to and to rectify data concerning them. Article 10 does not specify any exceptions, but does say that access and correction should be provided where necessary to "guarantee fair processing in respect of the data subject."

Specific provisions about access and correction were included in the Safe Harbor established by the U.S. Department of Commerce, after discussions with the European Union about how to transfer information lawfully to the United States.[19] The APEC Privacy Framework, discussed in Chapter 1, affirms the basic access principle that individuals should be able to obtain confirmation of whether or not the data controller holds personal information about them, and should gain access within a reasonable time and in a reasonable manner. The framework sets forth exceptions to the access and correction rights, with language similar to that in the Safe Harbor agreement:

> *Such access and opportunity for correction should be provided except where:*
> *i.   the burden or expense of doing so would be unreasonable or disproportionate to the risks to the individual's privacy;*
> *ii. the information should not be disclosed due to legal, security or commercial proprietary reasons; or,*
> *iii. the information privacy of persons other than the individual would be violated.*

In the event of a denial of access or correction request, the individual should be provided with reasons why and be able to challenge the denial.

In the United States, there is no general legal right for individuals to access or correct personal information held about them. Such rights do exist for personal health information covered by the HIPAA medical privacy rule. The Fair Credit Reporting Act also contains detailed access and correction provisions in order to prevent credit, employment or similar decisions being made based on incorrect personal information.

2.4 Online Security

Security administrators and hackers alike use software scripts to probe websites for security vulnerabilities—though with markedly different agendas.

A security administrator will use tools to identify system weaknesses so that these can be addressed and rectified.[20] However, an attacker can use similar tools to exploit weaknesses in order to gain unauthorized access to the web server.[21] In many respects, this has led to an "arms race" of technical weapons and tactics that pits "white hats" (security practitioners) against "black hats" (hackers and exploit artists).

The web facilitates information exchange between computers. While this gives further communication capability, it also exposes web servers and computers to greater risks. An organization should ensure that proper precautions are taken when it connects its computers to the Internet and the web. To take a familiar example, passwords should not be dictionary words, but rather a combination of letters, symbols, and numbers that hackers cannot easily guess.

2.4.1 Web Access

As discussed in detail in Chapter 4 ("Information Security"), an organization should have a comprehensive defense plan and a procedure in place to effectively address information security threats. All employees of the organization should be aware of the procedure, and the plan should extend to multiple areas and combat a variety of attack types. Also, the organization should anticipate that an attacker will utilize more than one method, so the design should have both the depth and the breadth to withstand sophisticated attacks.

These same information security principles apply in equal measure to an organization's website infrastructure. In many respects, websites are more vulnerable to compromise—both internal and external. Virtually every commercial entity in existence today employs at least one website as part of its business operations. These websites are, by design, externally facing and easily accessible through the use of a standard web browser application.

This sort of easy external visibility underscores the need for stringent web access policies. The more sensitive the website, the stronger the website authentication should be—requiring more than one form of access credential (e.g., two-factor authentication such as manual password plus token or ID card, also defined in Chapter 4). Further, consider deploying web forms that use the "password field" in HTML. This approach displays characters such as asterisks and bullets as text is entered, masking the actual characters entered.

Despite their use by website operators as identification mechanisms, web cookies offer imprecise means for authenticating and authorizing end user access. Cookies can be deleted or blocked by the user. This form of identification also lacks an accurate means of differentiating individual users of a single machine, such as when a device is used by multiple people in a household or by different scientists in a research laboratory.

2.4.2 Secure Sockets Layer and Transport Layer Security (SSL/TLS)

SSL/TLS, mentioned earlier in this chapter, is a standard method for encrypting the transmission of personally identifiable information over the web—including the verification of end user information required for website access.

SSL/TLS is a much stronger, higher-resolution scheme for data transmission. Though it does not rise to the security standard of PKI or other cryptographic schemes defined in Chapter 4, SSL/TLS is widely used for handling transmission of sensitive online data such as passwords or bank account numbers between web computers.

SSL/TLS gives the end user some level of comfort in the security of a web page delivery process. It also provides actual security if the web page hosting the web form is secured in SSL and the resulting data transmission supports the protocol.

2.4.3 Protecting Online Identity

Ultimately, individual end users are responsible for keeping their information private—and not disclosing it without appropriate consideration. Even if every website offers impeccable security, human error can lead to identity theft or data leaks. The following are standard practices to protect the privacy of information transmitted over the web:

- **Login/password/PINs.** Use unique passwords whenever possible, change passwords regularly, never set a system to "remember my password," and memorize passwords or keep them in secure storage rather than documenting them on paper or conveying them to others.

- **Software.** Use antivirus and firewall software and keep it up to date; also, keep the computer and server operating system software current, installing patches on a consistent basis.

- **Wireless networks (Wi-Fi) and Bluetooth.** Wireless communications are prone to interception by receivers near a Wi-Fi network or Bluetooth connection. In the cat-and-mouse game between attackers and computer security, there have been periods where attackers have been able to listen in on such wireless conversations. When deploying these technologies, update yourself on current vulnerabilities.

- **File sharing.** Be wary of peer-to-peer websites or services as these may give hackers or exploit artists an entry point into your computer. If you do use these services, utilize options made available to you to restrict what files and directories can be accessed by the website and services.

- **Public computers (in libraries, universities, airline lounges, hotel lobbies, etc.).** Be cautious of the information you provide through devices used by others, since you are not personally aware of how these machines have been configured, who has used them previously or what software (suspect or legitimate) they may host.

- **Personal information.** Be cautious about providing personal information unless you know the website is secure.

As identity theft has become more common and companies face legal liability for breaches of inadequately protected databases, more organizations are developing standards for the secure storage of personal information, whether the data is stored internally or via third parties such as subsidiaries and vendors.

The privacy and security ramifications of outsourcing information handling to third parties—as well as across geographic borders—were addressed in Chapter 4 ("Information Security").

2.4.4 E-mail Security

The principles of confidentiality, integrity and availability are as important in protecting e-mail as in any other area of web security or information security generally. Confidentiality of e-mail requires protecting it from unauthorized access. Integrity of e-mail involves a guarantee that it has not been modified or destroyed by an unauthorized individual. Availability of e-mail requires that mail servers remain online and able to service the user community.[22]

Some of the common features in mail security products today include content filtering services such as antivirus, antispam, HTML tag removal, script removal, blocking of attachments by file type, scanning of inappropriate content, confidentiality checks and disclaimer enforcement. Antispam methods supported by most products include real-time blackhole lists, heuristics, confirmation process, Bayesian filtering, open relay protection, size and bandwidth control and encryption.[23]

2.5 Children's Online Privacy

Many children access the Internet from an early age, raising several privacy issues distinct from the data collection and use issues relevant for adults. First, young children may not understand what data is being collected about them and how it is used. Second, even for children who might understand data collection and use, they cannot give meaningful "consent" to these activities as an adult can. In most countries, children cannot sign binding contracts, and thus meaningful consent to the collection and use of data must be obtained from parents or guardians. Third, children can easily fall victim to criminal behavior online. Unsuspecting young web users might reveal seemingly innocuous information to a "friend" online, such as details about their appearance, the name of their school or the location of their home—but a malicious web user can appropriate such information to criminal advantage.

One important source of protection for children is for parents to install filtering software on the household computer to block access to certain websites. Limits on a child's access also come from websites themselves. Many websites not designed for children require that the user be of a certain minimum age to access the site. For example, online retailers and adult entertainment sites can put restrictions on the ability of minors to access their products or services by requiring credit card information or proof of sufficient age.

In countries with comprehensive data protection regimes, there may be no specific laws governing collection and use of personal information from children. In such settings, general rules about "legitimate" processing of information may lead to more restrictive data practices concerning children. As discussed in Chapter 2, in the United States, the Children's Online Privacy Protection Act (COPPA) was passed specifically to protect children's use of the Internet—particularly websites and services targeted toward children. COPPA requires website operators to provide clear and conspicuous notice of the data collection methods employed by the website, including functioning hyperlinks to the website privacy policy on every web page where personal information is collected. It also requires consent by parents prior to collection of personal information for children under the age of 13.

However, neither the safeguards described throughout this book nor relevant privacy laws will completely prevent abuse of children's personal information online. Parents are advised to discuss web "dos and don'ts" with their children. Similarly, parents should become engaged in their children's online activities as well as be cognizant of emerging online threats.

2.6 Online Data Collection

The most common mechanism for capturing end user information online is through the use of web forms.

Figure 5-2: Web Form Soliciting User Information

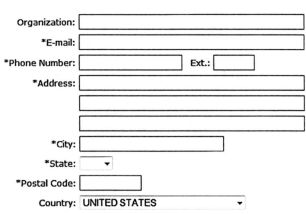

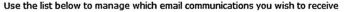

A **web form**, as shown in Figure 5-2, is a portion of a web page that contains blank fields, text boxes, check boxes or other input areas that end users complete by providing data (which may or may not include personal information).

- **One-line text boxes** are used to capture specific pieces of information such as name, city, credit card number or search terms. A label requesting a clear-cut entry is typically present. An important privacy consideration is that limitations should be placed on one-line text boxes to ensure that they are used only as intended (e.g., maximum of 14 characters for a first name). Otherwise, some attacks could result in data being withdrawn from the database instead of entered.

- **Scrolling text boxes** are used to capture a sentence or more of text. These are frequently used when an unspecified answer is desired. For instance, a common use is a request for support. Also, scrolling text boxes should be used with caution since little control exists over what information a user submits.

- **Check boxes and radio buttons** are used to collect answers to structured questions. Check boxes allow multiple answers to be selected out of a list of items, while radio buttons limit the user to one answer. Both options are more secure than fields that require the user to type text—the input is limited to the given options, and the content of the answer is not communicated over the web.

When the user completes and submits the web form, it is sent to a web server that processes and stores the submitted information in a database. This information may subsequently be used to process any number of user requests such as site entry, search queries or online transactions.

2.6.1 Active versus Passive Data Collection

Web forms commonly employ two methods of data collection: active and passive.

Active data collection occurs when the end user deliberately provides information to the website through the use of one of the input mechanisms described above.

Conversely, **passive data collection** occurs when information is gathered automatically— often without the end user's knowledge—as the user navigates from page to page on a website. This is typically accomplished through the use of web cookies or other types of identification mechanisms. (See Sections 2.9.1 and 2.9.2.)

Web forms should be designed to require only the information that is genuinely needed (and make it clear to the end user what, if anything, is optional). The end user may then provide only the personal information that is necessary for the transaction.

Further, the form input should be accompanied by a functioning link to the privacy statement (known formally as "notice at the point of collection"). The privacy statement should give the user a clear idea of how the data is used and who will have access to the information. The process that the user must undergo to view his data should be clear and explicit. One important consideration is that collection of sensitive personal information should be protected by use of secure transmission (e.g., SSL).

The auto-complete function of most web form submission processes should be disabled (or at least masked with asterisks or other obscuring characters) so that sensitive personal information is not exposed on shared computers (such as a machine used jointly by multiple family members for surfing the Web). To protect against account access by an unauthorized person, passwords should not be prepopulated in the web form.

A single sign-on service allows one universal service to confirm user authentication.[24] Only one sign-on is required per web session. This practice is risky if the user is on a public computer. Should he leave his station, another party could access information without proper authorization. A session should be set to time-out automatically to reduce this risk.

2.6.2 Desktop Products with Web Interfaces

Today, client software applications enable web-friendly capabilities such as active file types that support live sound and video. "Privacy by Design" should be built into these products at the development phase so the applications can be used safely and appropriately.

- **Office productivity applications** (e.g., word processors and spreadsheets) for many years resided principally on an individual's personal computer. Today, they are also provided through online cloud services such as GoogleDocs (see section 2.12 for further discussion about cloud technology). These products must ensure that the transmission to and from the cloud does not allow the data to leak into unprotected areas and risk capture by unauthorized persons.

- **Media player applications** allow music and video files to be played on a computer or mobile device. The player software must be discriminating in terms of the file formats and sources it imports and stores. For example, a past vulnerability allowed a false music file to be played that created a buffer overflow. Another concern has been the extent to which players allow the unauthorized copying and distribution of copyrighted material.[25]

- **Financial software** and services contain substantial amounts of confidential information. Such services are especially prone to attacks by criminals seeking to take money from accounts. Consequently, their protection is essential. When investigating reports of financial leaks in the past, the U.S. Government Accounting Office has evaluated features a company might use to control financial data. These include the ability to protect data and application programs from unauthorized access; prevent the introduction of unauthorized changes to application and system software; provide segregation of duties involving application programming, system programming, computer operations, information security and quality assurance; ensure recovery of computer processing operations in case of a disaster or other unexpected interruption; and ensure an adequate information security management program.[26]

2.6.3 Third-Party Interactions

The boundaries between websites are becoming blurred through the emergence of syndicated content, web services, co-branded online ventures, widgets and online advertising networks. Privacy professionals need to understand these third-party interactions and ensure that the appropriate privacy protections are in place. It should also be clear to end users which entities are capturing or receiving personal information in each of these scenarios—and that such entities accept accountability and fulfill their obligations under contract and applicable law.

Syndicated content is not actually created by the host site, but rather is developed by and/or purchased or licensed from outside sources such as news organizations. One concern with this type of web content is that it might contain malicious code that is then unwittingly incorporated into the organization's own website source code. For example, cross-site scripting (XSS) allows attackers to inject scripts into web pages for malicious purposes, taking advantage of the trust that users have for a given site.[27] The users' browsers may have settings that accept cookies or downloads from certain sites and not from others, but attacks such as XSS can smuggle code from such other sites.

Web services facilitate direct communication between computers.[28] They make it possible for organizations to interconnect with their suppliers online, or for users to get content from a site that has contracted with the site that the user has selected to visit. The linking organizations need to be particularly conscious of the information that is flowing between the computers, though, as the complexity of the system places both ends of the communication at a greater risk.

Co-branded sites are online partnerships between two or more content or service providers. Sharing of information is often allowed on co-branded sites, as long as it is disclosed in the privacy notice.

Online advertising networks connect online advertisers with web publishers that host advertisements on their sites. The networks enable media buyers to coordinate ad campaigns across sites. Through these targeted campaigns, advertisers can reach broad or focused audiences. Ad networks themselves vary in focus and size. Online advertising is discussed further later in this chapter.

Web widgets are applications that can be installed on a web page, blog, social profile or other HTML page. They typically are executed by the third party, although they appear on the page itself. The application can be executed by the owner of the page to deliver new website features or increased functionality. Widgets are frequently used as tools or content to make the site more dynamic.

Agent and vendor contracts present a unique set of issues. Language in contracts holding software vendors liable for problems that lead to security breaches is becoming more common. Similarly, the contracts may contain provisions that require notification of breaches that occur or patches that are available to repair the software.

2.6.4 Onward Transfers

A final consideration in online data collection is onward transfer of information from the original organization that holds the data to a third party. Onward transfers can occur in at least three settings.

Processors, as discussed in Chapter 1, are organizations that act on behalf of, and are subject to the direction of, the controller. For instance, the original website (the controller) hires accountants and may use a cloud service to store the data. The accountants and cloud service are processors, who act under the direction of the controller and should not use the data for purposes other than the controller's. The processors are able to use the data for their normal internal processes, such as their own management systems, but may not use the data for other purposes, such as marketing to the individuals. In most cases, controllers hire processors without the need to get consent from the individual data subject.

To complete the transaction, other organizations may receive and use data about the individual data subjects. Examples related to online commerce include a website's payment processor and a company that delivers packages to customers. Similar to processors, these organizations that complete the transaction generally cannot use the individuals' data for their own marketing purposes. In most cases, these organizations are hired by the website without the need for consent from the individual data subject.

Other third parties may also receive data to do their own marketing or for other purposes. For instance, the third party may receive data to conduct a sweepstakes or target marketing to the individuals. In many jurisdictions, including the European Union, the controller remains responsible for proper handling by third parties who receive personal information through onward transfer. In the United States, the Federal Trade Commission (FTC) considers onward transfer to be the responsibility of the host website—not the third party—and has issued guidance and brought enforcement actions toward this end.

Protection of personal information must be assured—contractually and procedurally—in data transfers between an organization's website and such third parties. Moreover, consumers must be explicitly notified when such transfers occur that (a) their personal information will be in the custody of a third party engaged by the host site, and (b) they have the ability to make a choice, typically by opting out, if they desire to prevent the onward transfer.

2.7 Online Attacks on Users

Internet users face attacks such as spam, phishing and spyware.

2.7.1 Spam E-mail

Spam is unsolicited commercial e-mail. The name is that of a packaged meat product and was first used in the early 1990s in response to an online mass marketing campaign by a U.S. immigration law firm. The firm distributed its message promoting the firm's legal services to thousands of Internet users. The Internet in that early period was not used for commercial activity. Longtime Internet users responded very negatively, and the term they used has become synonymous with unsolicited commercial messages online.

One obvious concern with spam is its sheer volume. In 2010, experts estimated that between 100 and 200 billion spam e-mails were sent globally each day, constituting over 80 percent of global e-mail according to 2011 estimates.[29] Spam clogs user inboxes, taking up the user's time and potentially overflowing available storage and bandwidth. In addition, spam e-mails can contain software viruses and other malicious code.

In response to this problem, e-mail providers and system operators today deploy sophisticated spam filters. Such filters often examine the content of e-mails to block messages containing known viruses and other malicious code. Where the sender or content of the e-mail seems likely to indicate spam, the filter can block delivery to the user entirely, or send such e-mails to a separate "likely spam" folder, which the user can review as desired. Spam filters are often configurable to different levels of strictness, and organizations or individual users can often "train" the spam filter over time to distinguish more accurately between spam and e-mails that users wish to receive.

Specific laws work together with such technical measures. As discussed in Chapter 2, in the United States, the CAN-SPAM Act requires a commercial e-mail to have a clear and conspicuous way for the user to unsubscribe from future e-mails. Since enactment of CAN-SPAM in 2003, reputable commercial companies must provide an easy way for users to prevent future e-mails from that company. Enforcement actions under CAN-SPAM have resulted in high fines and even jail sentences, pushing spammers out of the United States to other countries. In the European Union an opt-in consent system is used. Article 13(1) of the Directive on Privacy and Electronic Communications prohibits unsolicited commercial communications by e-mail, automated calling machines, fax or other electronic messaging system, unless the recipient provides prior consent. Exceptions exist for certain conditions. Article 13(4) prohibits sending anonymous electronic e-mails for the purpose of direct marketing in which recipients have no means of opting out of the e-mails. Recipients must be given an option to unsubscribe from these messages in each e-mail sent.

Many business groups have codes of conduct and self-regulatory frameworks in place for commercial e-mail. Common commercial e-mail principles include:

- No false or misleading header information
- No deceptive subject lines
- Opt-out mechanism in each message
- Notification that the message contains an advertisement or promotional information
- Information about the sending organization

2.7.2 Phishing

Phishing is the practice of sending a spam e-mail that lures users to a fake website in order to fraudulently capture sensitive personal information. These e-mails appear to originate from legitimate organizations—such as recognized banks or retailers—and may include seemingly legitimate trademarks, colors, logos or other corporate signatures. Users are asked to follow a link to confirm their account number, credit card details or other sensitive or personal information. The link takes the users to a forged website that records the data that they enter. The perpetrators can then resell the personal information or use it for illegal activities such as bank fraud or identity theft.

Phishing to perpetrate theft is a crime, and not simply an annoyance or technical threat. According to a 2005 SANS Institute whitepaper:

> For the most part, a phishing attack is easy and cheap to engineer, is extremely hard to trace, and even if only a small percentage of recipients respond to requests for personal information—the return on investment can be very high. Sending an email costs a fraction of a cent, and minimal response can result in high returns.[30]

Early phishing attacks were often crudely done, containing typographic and syntax errors and bad imitations of a famous logo. Over time, the quality of the fake e-mails has improved, so that even a sophisticated recipient might believe that the e-mail is from a genuine source.

Spear phishing is a more sophisticated variation on the earlier type of phishing, which was a mass spam e-mail that imitated a widely used brand name. With spear phishing, the perpetrator crafts an e-mail that specifically targets the recipient—instead of a phishing "net" that scoops up a lot of victims, the spear phishing attack is pointed at a particular victim. For instance, the message may appear to come from the recipient's boss, or from someone who has recently been in a meeting with the recipient.

2.7.3 Spyware

Spyware is software that is downloaded covertly, without the end user understanding or consenting to the actions of the software. Spyware is used to fraudulently collect and use sensitive personal information such as bank account credentials and credit card numbers. Some spyware, for instance, can report each keystroke by a user back to the entity that controls the spyware. Spyware is often installed by "drive-by downloads," where the user never provides consent to the download or is tricked into downloading the software, such as when spyware is bundled with other software that the user wishes to download. (See Figure 5-3 for an example of a fraudulent spyware message.)

Figure 5-3: False Security Warning

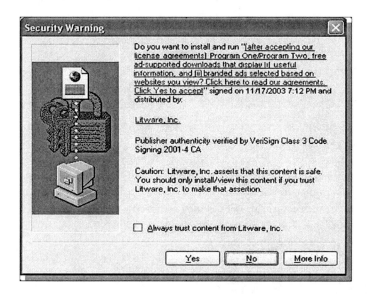

There is no simple distinction between illegal or inappropriate spyware, and legitimate software that performs user activity monitoring as intended. For instance, a user might wish to have software that allows someone at a remote location to read what is on the screen, such as when a computer user receives technical help from a technician who can see the user's screen or each keystroke. Spyware thus cannot be defined by the technical act of sending personal information from the user's computer to a remote computer. Instead, the definition of spyware depends in large part on the intent and knowledge of the user, and whether it is reasonable to believe that the user wished to have the information transmitted back to the remote location.

2.8 Online Verification and Certification

Verifying and certifying privacy protections is one way to enhance users' level of trust in online activity. The verification or certification is done by third-party organizations, known as accreditation or assurance services, or trust seal providers. The third parties evaluate activities, such as the privacy notices of a website, or confirm the absence of viruses or spyware from a software download. The activities are evaluated against predefined industry standards and best practices. Where compliance exists, the third parties then grant the certification. For instance, the third party's name and seal may appear on a website or next to the download link for software.

TRUSTe, VeriSign and BBBOnline are three examples of third parties that provide online verification and certification services. Each offers an accreditation that sets standards for receiving a trust mark and also provides an independent dispute resolution process in the event of a privacy abuse alleged by an online consumer.

Other self-regulatory regimes include the Network Advertising Initiative, the U.S. Direct Marketing Association, the Japan Information Processing Development Center, EuroPriSe, the Health Information Trust Alliance and American Institute of CPAs.

2.9 Targeted Online Advertising and Web User Tracking

Many websites rely on online advertising to fund their services to customers. As technology has evolved, there have been extensive public debates about the proper rules and procedures for targeted online advertising.[31] Proponents of targeted advertising emphasize how it provides value to both the web user and the website operator. Users benefit by seeing more relevant content and advertising, and higher ad revenues support a wider range of free content on the Internet. Targeted advertisements support the websites themselves as well as the ecosystem of advertising and other companies that provide support services for websites.

On the other hand, privacy advocates and some regulators have expressed concerns about targeted online advertising. Concerns include that individuals receive unclear notice and often do not know how to choose whether to receive targeted advertisements. When individuals visit a website, they are often unaware that their browsing habits may be tracked by third-party advertising networks. Although industry has provided mechanisms for opting out of such networks, regulators have questioned the effectiveness of such mechanisms. The FTC and others have suggested a "Do Not Track" approach, which would allow individuals to make a single choice not to be subjected to targeted online advertising.[32] A prominent self-regulatory effort invloves the Digital Advertising Alliance, a coalition of media and advertising organizations that has developed an icon program that users click on to obtain information on how to exercise choice with respect to online behavioral advertising. In Europe, Directive 2009/136/EC, also known as the EU Cookie Directive, requires that users give consent before having cookies (see Section 2.9.1) placed on their computers, thereby preventing any tracking of their online activities if they do not "opt in." (Figure 5-5 shows an example of a cookie prompt.)

In addition to advertising techniques such as pop-up ads and "adware," much online advertising has depended on technologies such as cookies, which help a website or advertising network track a user's browsing activities, potentially across multiple websites visited.

Pop-up ads are advertising messages that appear to the end user in a separate browser window in response to browsing behavior or viewing of a site. Pop-up ads were a major advertising technique early in the development of online commerce, but are less prominent today, in part because major web browsers block pop-up ads by default or through easy-to-use controls. Pop-up ads have also sometimes been a symptom of greater problems, such as spyware or other malware.[33]

Adware is software that is installed on a user's computer, often bundled with freeware (free software), such as peer-to-peer file-sharing programs or online games. It monitors the end user's online behavior so that additional advertising can be targeted to that person based on his or her specific interests and behaviors. Unless there is clear consent by users to this monitoring, however, such adware may be considered spyware by privacy enforcement agencies.

2.9.1 Web Cookies

The word *cookie* comes from "magic cookie," a term in programming languages for a piece of information shared between cooperating pieces of software. Cookies are widely used on the Internet to enable someone other than the user to link a computing device to previous web actions by the same device. The standard cookie, or HTML cookie, is a small text file that a web server places on the hard drive of a user's computer. Cookies enable a range of functions, including authentication of web visitors, personalization of content and delivery of targeted advertising. There have been ongoing privacy debates, however, about what constitutes appropriate notice and choice for users for cookies placed on their hard drives.

Figure 5-4: Cookie Prompt in Microsoft Internet Explorer

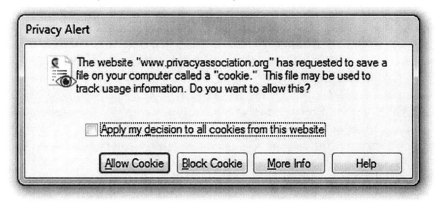

Used with permission from Microsoft.

For purposes of privacy compliance, an ongoing issue has been when and whether information contained in cookies should be considered personal information. In some usage cases, the information clearly is personal information; for instance, a website may have an identified transaction with a user, such as a credit card purchase that shows the user's name. If that credit card purchase is linked in the company's database with the information collected through cookies, then all of the information is identifiable. In other settings, however, no name is directly linked to a cookie. The cookie might indicate that a particular computer has visited the same website on several occasions, or show that the same computer has visited a list of different websites. The organization that sets the cookie, however, may have no indication of the name or other identifying information associated with that computer.

The EU, in its Electronic Privacy Directive of 2002, has taken the position that information stored in cookies is generally "personal data," so that individual consent is needed before the cookie can be placed on a user's hard drive. How and when to implement such consent has been the topic of ongoing uncertainty, including for websites that operate outside of the EU but have EU visitors.

In recognition of possible privacy issues related to cookies, web browsers have created user controls for cookies. Individuals can thus choose when to have explicit notice that a cookie is being set, can view cookies stored on their hard drive and can choose whether or not to permit cookies to be set by default. Users can also delete the cookies stored on their hard drive.

From a best practices standpoint, web cookies should:

- Not store unencrypted personal information

- Provide adequate notice of their usage

- Use a persistent variation only if the need justifies it (see below)

- Not set long expiration dates

- Disclose the involvement of a third-party cookie provider (if applicable) as well as an opt-out (or in Europe, an opt-in) mechanism for delivery from that third party

Several varieties of the standard web cookie files, also known as HTML cookies, exist and are used widely on the web. These include session-based and persistent cookies (relating to the time and duration of cookie deployment) as well as first-party and third-party cookies (relating to the origination point of cookie file delivery).

A *session cookie* is stored only while the user is connected to the particular web server—the cookie is deleted when the user leaves that website or closes the web browser. Session cookies address a basic problem—a website has no way to know automatically that it is the same device, operated for the same user, that asks for one page after another. For instance, session cookies are used in "shopping carts"—the way that an online user first selects one or more items from an online store, and then goes to another page on the site to pay and arrange delivery. Without a cookie, the website has no easy and effective way to know that each item in the shopping cart is for the same user, and to have the contents of the shopping cart, when complete, be listed for payment. Other common uses of session cookies include managing chat sessions (to ensure that the same device sends and receives messages for each user name) and supporting interactive opinion surveys conducted by market research organizations. Because session cookies expire when the browser closes, they do not identify a device over time, and so have not been the subject of most privacy debates about cookies.[34]

A *persistent cookie* is set to expire at some point in the future, from a few minutes to days or even years from initial delivery. Until expiration, the organization that set the cookie can recognize that it is the same cookie on the same device, and thus often the same user, that earlier visited the website.

The use of persistent cookies has expanded significantly over time. They are the standard mechanism for authenticating return visitors to websites where a user has an account, including social networking sites, music sites, e-commerce sites and many other sites. Persistent cookies enable "personalization," so that the website displays different content or in a different format based on prior interactions with that site. For instance, a news site might be personalized to feature news about a person's favorite sports teams or other topics of interest. Persistent cookies are also used by online advertising networks to recognize when the same device has visited one of the websites that has a contract with that network. The advertising network may keep a history of what ads have previously been sent to that device, and can tailor subsequent ads based on this history.

A *first-party cookie* is set and read by the web server hosting the website the user is visiting. For instance, an online retailer or government agency can set a first-party cookie on the hard drive of a user who chooses to visit the retailer's or agency's site.

Conversely, a *third-party cookie* is set and read by or on behalf of a party other than the web server that is providing a service. (The "second party" is understood to be the user who is surfing the web.) Online advertising networks set third-party cookies, as do companies that provide analytics of web usage across sites. Some websites enable "widgets" or other software that appears on the first party's website, but interacts with a third party, which may set a third-party cookie.

A *Flash cookie* is contrasted with the standard cookies discussed thus far, which are more specifically known as HTML cookies. Flash cookies are stored and accessed by Adobe Flash, a browser plug-in commonly used by many Internet sites. While online, an individual's Internet browser collects and stores information from sites visited in the form of cache, or cookies. Traditional HTML cookies, as previously discussed in this chapter, can be deleted. A Flash cookie, however, is stored outside the Internet browser's control, meaning that individuals cannot delete the Flash cookies directly through the browser. Additionally, individuals are not notified when Flash cookies are stored, and these cookies do not expire. Flash cookies can be used to track an individual's actions and to store the same information stored in a normal HTML cookie. Thus, when an individual deletes the HTML cookie, websites can use the Flash cookies to "respawn" the information that was stored in the HTML cookie. This raises serious privacy implications for individuals, who under current technology have little control over the use of such cookies, and whose privacy choices about cookies can thus be circumvented.

2.9.2 Web Beacons

Another online identification mechanism is called a web beacon. Known also as a web bug, pixel tag or clear GIF, a web beacon is a clear graphic image of a 1x1 pixel that is delivered through a web browser or HTML-compliant e-mail client application to an end user's computer—usually as part of a web page request or in an HTML e-mail message, respectively.

The web beacon operates as a tag that records an end user's visit to a particular web page. It is also often used in conjunction with a web cookie and provided as part of a third-party tracking service. Web beacons provide an ability to produce specific profiles of user behavior in combination with web server logs. Common usage scenarios for web beacons include online ad impression counting, file download monitoring and ad campaign performance management (click-through rates, ad frequency limitation, etc.). Web beacons also can report to the sender about which e-mails are read by recipients.

Privacy considerations for web beacons are similar to those for cookies, notably how to meet a jurisdiction's requirements. Some sort of notice is important because the clear pixel of a web beacon is quite literally invisible to the end user.

2.9.3 Digital Fingerprinting

Digital fingerprinting can identify a device based on information revealed to the website by the user. When a web page is requested, there is no automatic identification of who is seeking to download the content. The web server, though, typically receives certain information connected to the request, and maintains logs, which are used for security and system maintenance purposes. These log files generally include the IP address of the visitor, the date and time stamp of the page request, the URL of the requested page or file, the URL the visitor came from immediately prior to the visit (e.g., the referrer URL), the visitor's web browser type version and the web user's computer operating system.

The website also receives more detailed information, such as the particular fonts used by the requesting computer, which can in some cases be used to "fingerprint" a device. This more detailed information varies enough among computing devices that two devices are unlikely to be the same. This digital fingerprinting has been used as a security technique by financial and other institutions so that an account holder is asked for additional security assurances before logging on from a new device. In contrast to this security benefit, some privacy enforcement agencies have questioned what would constitute sufficient notice and consent for digital fingerprinting techniques to be used for targeted advertising.

2.10 Search Engines

Specific issues about search engine privacy have been raised by regulators and privacy advocates. The use of personal information in connection with search engines is important because of the central role that search engines perform in how people access information on the Internet. When using cookies or other tracking techniques, the issues concerning search engines are generally similar to those for cookies, as discussed above.

Some privacy issues, however, are more specific to search engines. The content of the search may give clues about a searcher's identity, such as through "vanity" searches (where users look up their own names), as may search patterns around a person's address or workplace. The content of searches may also include information considered sensitive for privacy purposes in a particular country, such as medical information or a person's political views. To address such concerns, major search engines have adopted measures to anonymize searches after a defined period, such as an agreed-upon number of months.

2.11 Online Social Networking

Online social networks are services or platforms that build on, and expand, traditional social networks established in everyday life. These websites establish forums for connecting with friends, family, colleagues and others. Popular social networks include Facebook, Twitter and LinkedIn. While their technological features are similar, the cultures of different social networks are varied. Some sites enhance preexisting social networks; others allow strangers to connect based on shared interests or views. Some social networks cater to large and diverse populations, such as Facebook. Others are targeted at specific audiences with similar interests or affiliations. Many sites incorporate communication tools, file and media sharing capability, and blogging features and allow for mobile access.

Social networks have grown recently and rapidly. For instance, Facebook opened to the general public in 2006, but had over 845 million users globally in 2011.[35] Online social networks are valuable for facilitating the exchange of information and increasing global connectivity, and have become platforms for online games, specialized marketing campaigns, and an increasing array of activities.

These new activities, however, carry with them new privacy concerns. The individual has tools for controlling his or her visibility on these networks; however, privacy control mechanisms are not consistent and still evolving. Privacy vulnerabilities include the transmittance of personal information to unwanted third parties, such as potential employers, law enforcement, or strangers. Information can potentially be passed on or sold to advertisers and intruders may steal passwords or other unencrypted data. Privacy and security standards and best practices are likely to evolve with the continued rapid expansion of online social networks.

2.12 Cloud Computing

The term "cloud" is derived from computer network diagrams, which depict the Internet as a large cloud shape, because the many computer components in a network are too numerous to be illustrated individually. Cloud computing refers to the storage, processing, and access to data and applications on remote servers accessible by the Internet, rather than on a single computer or network.[36] Thus, users have on-demand access to their data or applications wherever they can access the Internet. There are five essential characteristics of cloud computing, three service models, and four deployment models.[37]

The Five Essential Characteristics of Cloud Computing

1. **On-demand self-service.** Users must be able to access their cloud resources without having to first consult with the cloud provider.

2. **Broad network access.** Cloud computing is network based and available from any standard platform, such as a computer or mobile device.

3. **Resource pooling.** The computing resources in the cloud are shared, meaning that many clients may use the same resources at the same time.

4. **Rapid elasticity.** Cloud computing is easily scaled up or down to adjust for demand.

5. **Measured service.** Similar to utility providers, cloud providers must measure the cloud service provided and respond accordingly, in terms of billing and technology updates.

The Three Service Models of Cloud Computing

1. **Cloud software as a service (SaaS).** SaaS cloud computing performs software functions that would previously have been installed and run on a desktop computer or other device. With SaaS, the cloud provider hosts the software so that the user does not need to install or manage it and does not even need to purchase the hardware.

2. **Cloud platform as a service (PaaS).** PaaS provides a service through which web developers build and publish applications using the cloud provider's cloud infrastructure.

3. **Cloud infrastructure as a service (IaaS).** IaaS providers own and maintain key computing resources that users rent. The providers rent users web storage, network capacity and other resources.

The Four Deployment Models of Cloud Computing

1. In a **private cloud**, the infrastructure is owned or leased by a single organization.

2. In a **public cloud**, large-scale infrastructure is available and sold to the public on a self-service basis.

3. A **community cloud** infrastructure is shared between organizations in a specific community.

4. The **hybrid cloud** is an infrastructure composed of two or more clouds.

The widespread and growing use of cloud computing introduces new privacy and security concerns. Storing sensitive and personal information on the cloud means that large amounts of data are held in one location, so that one breach can have a large effect. Some cloud providers encrypt the data stored on their servers, but others leave data in plain text and thus more vulnerable to data breaches. There is also the concern that cloud service providers will disclose user data to third parties for marketing or advertising purposes, or in response to government requests for information. On the other hand, security may also be increased because cloud computing can provide organizations with better and more comprehensive data protection mechanisms that cover all data stored in the cloud.

2.13 Mobile Online Privacy

The use of mobile devices, often connected to the Internet, has expanded enormously in recent years. Mobile devices such as smartphones, cell phones and tablet computers empower individuals, bringing the advantages of the Internet to daily life. Users have rapidly become accustomed to previously unheard of capabilities, from accessing real-time maps while driving to asking questions of search engines during social or business events. Today's mobile devices are powerful and complex machines, capable of running operating systems and applications that previously were available to individuals primarily through desktop computers.

Mobile devices also present new privacy and security challenges. Particularly important is the issue of geo-location data. Individuals often carry their mobile phones and tablet computers with them during the day. These devices enable tracking of the user's movements, a category of personal information that typically did not exist before users owned mobile devices. One set of privacy issues concerns the proper rules for collection, use and storage of location data by mobile phone companies or others who are authorized to know the location of the device in order to provide mobile service. An additional set of privacy issues concerns the ability of other parties to access that location data, or to pay those with location data to place advertisements. Analysts expect location-based services (LBS) to expand rapidly in the coming years.[38] LBS inform users about things they can do or purchase close to their current location. LBS also present new business opportunities for local businesses and for the intermediaries that link users to businesses, but privacy and security best practices will need to be developed for this evolving industry.

Improved privacy and user-consent mechanisms will likely develop as the mobile ecosystem matures. Presenting effective notice can become more difficult on smartphone screens, which are typically much smaller than the screens for desktops or laptops. Best practices will need to develop for individual choice, including which parties receive location data and in what level of detail (such as a city, neighborhood or specific address). One challenge is that it is difficult to anonymize location data—people return often to their homes and workplaces, allowing linkage of location data with identity. As mobile devices continue to grow in use and power, so too will the complexity of mobile privacy issues.

3. Summary

The continued growth and success of the Internet is due largely to its increasing popularity as a platform for electronic communications, commerce and information exchange. Not surprisingly, privacy and security considerations abound. Web consumers accustomed to submitting information to various service providers in order to obtain desired features and services must be more vigilant about the release of such information. Website operators have a number of legal and practical obligations to ensure that they are capturing personal information for reasonable business purposes and with appropriate notice and choice to the consumer. Legislators and privacy advocates will continue to press for more controls on what information is tracked on the Internet, with the ability for users to make a conscious choice on what information is collected on them, by whom and for what purposes.

Endnotes

1   Jack L. Brock Jr. and Keith A. Rhodes, *Testimony Before the Permanent Subcommittee on Investigations, Committee on Governmental Affairs, U.S. Senate, Information Security: Computer Hacker Information Available on the Internet,* June 5, 1996, www.gao.gov/archive/1996/ai96108t.pdf.

2   NASA, "Web Accessibility Best Practices from NASA Webmaster Community," www.hq.nasa.gov/webaccess/AccessibilityBestPractice.htm.

3   www.w3.org/2011/02/htmlwg-pr.html.

4   Paul Madsen and Carlisle Adams, XML.com, "Privacy and XML," Part I, April 17, 2002, www.xml.com/pub/a/2002/04/17/privacy.html.

5   GAO, *Technology Assessment: Cybersecurity for Critical Infrastructure Protection,* May 2004, 151, www.gao.gov/new.items/d04321.pdf.

6   ICANN controls the creation of top-level domains. (The application can be viewed at ICANN's website, www.icann.org.)

7   Federal Trade Commission, "Children's Online Privacy Protection Rule—Comment, P994504," Comments of the Center for Democracy and Technology, June 11, 1999, www.ftc.gov/privacy/comments/cdt.htm.

8   Children's Online Privacy Protection Rule, 16 C.F.R. Part 312, April 21, 2000, www.ftc.gov/os/1999/10/childrensprivacy.pdf.

9   Alan O. Freier, Philip Karlton and Paul C. Kocher, "The SSL Protocol Version 3.0," November 1999, www.mozilla.org/projects/security/pki/nss/ssl/draft302.txt.

10 *Id.*

11 www.quirksmode.org/js/intro.html.

12 Thomas Powell and Fritz Schneider, "JavaScript Security," in *JavaScript: The Complete Reference,* 2d ed. (Berkeley, CA: Osborne/McGraw-Hill, 2004).

13 Matteo Campofiorito, "OneITSecurity, Pwn2Own 2010," interview with Charlie Miller, March 1, 2010, www.oneitsecurity.it/01/03/2010/interview-with-charlie-miller-pwn2own/.

14 http://blogs.adobe.com/conversations/2011/11/flash-focus.html.

15 TRUSTe, "TRUSTe Guidance on Model Website Disclosures," www.truste.org/docs/Model_Privacy_Policy_Disclosures.doc.

16 Janlori Goldman, Health Privacy Project, *Testimony Before the U.S. House of Representatives Subcommittee on Government Management, Information, and Technology of the Committee on Government Reform and Oversight on "The Consumer Protection and Medical Record Confidentiality Act of 1998,"* May 14, 1998, 6, www.cdt.org/files/file/33815_0.pdf.

17 Privacy Act of 1974, 5 U.S.C. §552a, (1974), www.justice.gov/opcl/privstat.htm.

18 *Id.*

19 *Id.* See also BBBOnline, European Union/U.S. Safe Harbor Compliance, www.bbb.org/us/european-dispute-resolution/; U.S. Department of Commerce, Safe Harbor Overview, http://export.gov/safeharbor/eu/eg_main_018476.asp; European Union, Directive 2002/58/EC, July 12, 2002, http://eur-lex.europa.eu/LexUriServ/LexUriServ.do?uri=OJ:L:2002:201:0037:0037:EN:PDF.

20 Justin Pope, *Haunted By Ghosts Of Hard Drives Past,* Jan. 16, 2003, at www.cbsnews.com/stories/2003/01/16/tech/main536774.shtml.

21 *Id.*

22 Pam Cocca, "Email Security Threats," Sept. 20, 2004, 3, www.sans.org/reading_room/whitepapers/email/email-security-threats_1540.

23 *Id.*

24 Patrick McDaniel, "Computer and Network Authentication," September 18, 2006, www.patrickmcdaniel.org/pubs/mcdaniel-netauth.pdf.

25 "RealNetworks Patches Media-Player Vulnerabilities: After Confirming Three Flaws Uncovered in U.K.," *TechBuilder.org,* Feb. 6, 2004, www.technewsworld.com/story/32797.html.

26 GAO, "Information Security: Weak Controls Place Interior's Financial and Other Data at Risk," July 3, 2001, 14, www.iwar.org.uk/comsec/resources/gao/d01615.pdf.

27 PHP Security Consortium, *PHP Security Guide,* Nov. 14, 2004, 14, http://shiflett.org/php-security.pdf.

28 GAO, *Technology Assessment,* 118.

29 Daren Lewis, "The Recent Drop in Global Spam Volumes—What Happened?" Symantec.com, Oct. 6, 2010, www.symantec.com/connect/blogs/recent-drop-global-spam-volumes-what-happened.

30 Cocca, "Email Security Threats," www.sans.org/reading_room/whitepapers/email/email-security-threats_1540.

31 Julia Angwin, "Stealthy Tracking Tools Raise Questions About Self-Regulation," *Wall Street Journal,* August 18, 2011, http://blogs.wsj.com/digits/2011/08/18/stealthy-tracking-tools-raise-questions-about-self-regulation/.

32 FTC, Preliminary FTC Staff Report, "Protecting Consumer Privacy in an Era of Rapid Change," Dec. 2010, www.ftc.gov/os/2010/12/101201privacyreport.pdf.

33 Jerry Berman, Center for Democracy and Technology, *Testimony Before the Senate Committee on Commerce, Science, and Transportation Subcommittee on Communications on the SPY BLOCK Act,* March 23, 2004, http://old.cdt.org/testimony/20040323berman.shtml.

34 GAO, "Internet Privacy: Implementation of Federal Guidance for Agency Use of 'Cookies,'" Report to the Chairman, Committee on Governmental Affairs, U.S. Senate, April 2001, www.gao.gov/new.items/d01424.pdf.

35 Statistics, Facebook.com, last accessed February 22, 2012, http://newsroom.fb.com/content/default. aspx?NewsAreaId=22.

36 The "cloud" in "cloud computing" is derived from the use of the cloud as a metaphor for the on-line network, and is often depicted as a cartoon cloud. See Jessie Holliday Scanlon and Brad Wieners, "Guest Column: The Internet Cloud," *Computerworld*, July 16, 1999, www.computerworld.com.au/article/104942/guest_column_internet_cloud/.

37 Peter Mell and Tim Grance, National Institute of Standards and Technology, "The NIST Definition of Cloud Computing," September 2011, http://csrc.nist.gov/publications/nistpubs/800-145/SP800-145. pdf.

38 The market for location-based services is predicted to exceed $12 billion by 2014. "Mobile Location-Based Services Market to Exceed $12bn by 2014 Driven by Increased Apps Store Usage, Smartphone Adoption and New Hybrid Positioning Technologies, According to Juniper Research, 2010," press release, www.juniperresearch.com/viewpressrelease.php?id=213&pr=180.

Index

About the Authors

Peter P. Swire, CIPP/US

Peter Swire is the C. William O'Neill Professor of Law at The Ohio State University, a senior fellow at the Future of Privacy Forum and the Center for American Progress, and policy fellow at the Center for Democracy and Technology.

Swire has been a leading scholar, government leader and practitioner in privacy since the 1990s. Under President Clinton, Swire served in the White House as the chief counselor for privacy in the Office of Management and Budget, where he had U.S. government-wide responsibility for privacy policy. In that role, he was the White House coordinator for the proposed and final HIPAA medical privacy rules and chaired a White House task force on how to update wiretap laws for the Internet age. He also participated in the negotiation of the Safe Harbor agreement for trans-border data flows between the EU and the United States.

Swire returned to the White House in 2009 and 2010, serving as special assistant to President Obama for economic policy, working in the National Economic Council under Lawrence Summers.

He has written three books and numerous scholarly articles on privacy and cyber security (many of his writings and speeches are available at www.peterswire.net) and has served on privacy and security advisory boards for companies including Google, IBM, Intel and Microsoft. For eight years he was a consultant with the global law firm of Morrison & Foerster, LLP.

Swire graduated from Princeton University, summa cum laude, and the Yale Law School, where he was an editor of the *Yale Law Journal*.

Kenesa Ahmad, CIPP/US, LLM

Kenesa Ahmad is an information privacy attorney and co-author of *U.S. Private-sector Privacy: Law and Practice for Information Privacy Professionals*. Ahmad received her law degree from the Moritz College of Law of The Ohio State University, where she served as an articles editor of the *Ohio State Law Journal*. She also received her LLM from Northwestern University Law School. From 2011–2012 Ahmad completed a legal and policy fellowship with the Future of Privacy Forum. She is now an associate in the global privacy practice of Promontory Financial Group.

Managing Editor

Terry McQuay, CIPP/US, CIPP/C, CIPP/E, CIPP/G

Terry McQuay is president and founder of Nymity Inc. He is a fellow for the Ponemon Institute and is on the Advisory Council for the Future of Privacy Forum. McQuay is a member of the Centre for Information Policy Leadership and a Privacy by Design Ambassador. He is involved with the United States Council for International Business and the International Chamber of Commerce and attends Organisation for Economic Co-operation and Development and Asia-Pacific Economic Cooperation privacy meetings.

Contributing Editors

Blaine Currie, CIPP/US, MBA, PhD

Blaine Currie is a privacy legal researcher at Nymity Inc. and has worked in the research department for the past year. Prior to working at Nymity, Currie was privacy officer and vice president of operations at Maritz Inc.

Lara Hunt

Lara Hunt is a privacy legal researcher at Nymity Inc. and has worked in the research department for over two years. Hunt came to Nymity with over 20 years' experience in the retail sector, including the areas of privacy, communications, operations and human resources.

John Jager, CIPP/US, CIPP/C, CIPP/G

John Jager is vice president, research services at Nymity Inc. and has been with the Nymity team since 2006. Prior to joining Nymity, Jager was chief privacy officer at Sears Canada and has been actively involved in the privacy committees at the Canadian Marketing Association and Retail Council of Canada.

Meaghan McCluskey, CIPP/US, CIPP/E, LLB

Meaghan McCluskey is the senior privacy research lawyer at Nymity Inc. and has worked in the research department for over three years. Prior to working at Nymity, McCluskey was an articling student in the legal department of the Office of the Information and Privacy Commissioner of Ontario.

Camille McQuay, CIPP/US, CIPP/E, CIPP/G, LLB

Camille McQuay is vice president, research at Nymity, Inc. and has led the research department for over six years. Prior to working at Nymity, McQuay was general counsel at Desnoes & Geddes Ltd. (now Red Stripe) and a member of the Kraft Inc. legal team.

Nymity Inc.

Nymity Inc. enables responsible organizations (public and private sector, enterprise-size or small business) to effectively maintain compliance with privacy and data protection laws around the world. Nymity's solutions also allow responsible organizations to demonstrate both compliance and accountability with an evidence-based reporting tool.

Nymity is an online solutions partner for accountability to hundreds of organizations around the world complying with local legislation or utilizing frameworks such as Binding Corporate Rules, Safe Harbor, Cross-Border Privacy Rules, Generally Accepted Privacy Principles or the Privacy Maturity Model.